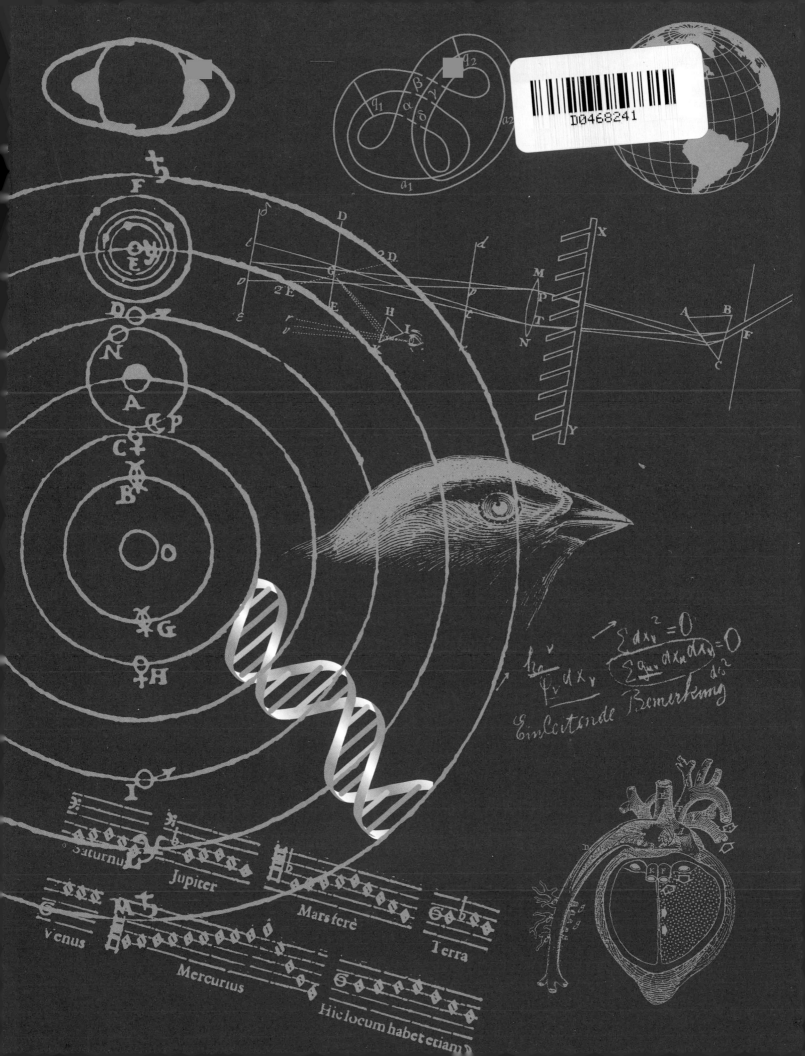

SCIENTIFIC GENIUS

THE TWENTY GREATEST MINDS

SCIENTIFIC GENIUS

THE TWENTY GREATEST MINDS

JIM GLENN

Saraband

Published by Saraband Inc.
PO Box 0032, Rowayton, CT
06853-0032, USA

ISBN 1-887354-05-0

10 9 8 7 6 5 4 3 2 1

Printed in China

Edited by Robin Langley Sommer and Gail Janensch
Design © Ziga Design
Scientific illustrations © 1996 by Fern Hamilton
Picture research by Gillian Speeth
Graphics © 1996 by Chris Berlingo

Below: Robert Koch at a South African field laboratory, laboring to isolate the virus responsible for rinderpest.

The publisher would like to thank Claire Gordon for preparing the index; Emily Head for editorial assistance; and the following individuals and institutions for supplying illustrations on the pages listed:

AKG London: 10, 48; **American Association for the Advancement of Science:** 144 (top, reprinted from *Science*, volume 119, page 620, Figure 1); **© 1994 Aris Multimedia Entertainment Inc.:** 78 (center, photo by Tom Atwood); **Bassano Studios:** 136; **© 1996 Chris Berlingo:** 124, 143; **The Bettmann Archive:** 8, 11, 14 (top), 16 (bottom), 21, 22, 24 (bottom left), 25 (bottom), 26 (both), 28 (bottom), 30, 31, 33, 36 (both), 37 (top), 39, 45, 46 (top), 50, 51, 52, 53 (top), 58, 67, 68, 75, 77, 79 (bottom), 86 (bottom), 90, 91, 99, 100, 101 (top), 104 (both), 105 (both), 110, 112, 126, 133, 139 (bottom); **British Film Institute, Department of Stills, Posters and Designs:** 139 (top); **CorelDraw:** 97; **© 1996 M.C. Escher/Cordon Art, Baarn, Holland:** 115; **The Field Museum:** 82 (photo by Ron Testa, neg # GEO 84968); 83 (photo by John Weinstein, neg # GN86962.5); **© 1996 Fern Hamilton:** 14 (bottom), 15 (top), 19, 40, 54 (both), 63, 71, 87, 113, 117, 120, 121, 135, 138, 147; **© International Business Machines Corporation:** 131 (bottom), 134 (top, center, bottom right); **Mendelianum Museum Moraviae, Brno:** 92, 94; **The MIT Museum:** 134 (bottom left); **NASA:** 27 (bottom), 57 (bottom), 148; **National Optical Astronomy Observatories:** 151; **National Center for Supercomputing Applications, University of Illinois at Urbana-Champaign:** 152–153 (all); **© 1996 Jay Olstad:** 78 (top and bottom); **Peter E. Palmquist:** 96; **Images © 1996 by PhotoDisc Inc:** 15 (bottom), 27 (top), 37 (center & bottom), 55 (both), 57 (top), 86 (top), 101 (bottom); **Prints and Photographs Division, Library of Congress:** 12, 13, 20, 23, 28 (top), 29 (top), 35, 44, 47, 61, 64, 66, 72, 74, 76, 98, 102, 103, 106, 107, 108, 109 (both), 114, 122, 123, 129; **Reuters/Bettmann:** 149, 154; **Science Museum, London:** 46 (center & bottom); **David Eugene Smith Portrait Collection, Rare Book and Manuscript Library, Columbia University:** 85; **University of Manchester:** 137 (both), 140 (photos by Mike Koiston); **UPI/Bettmann Newsphotos:** 80, 81, 116, 118, 130, 131 (top), 142, 144 (bottom), 145 (both), 146; **US Department of Agriculture:** 95; **US Dept of Energy:** 73; **Ullstein Bilderdienst, Berlin:** 125; **Yerke's Observatory, University of Chicago:** 24 (bottom right).

Foreword

No one has really been able to pin down what we mean by "genius." Sometimes it's associated with the notion of intelligence, but that's a conceptual roller coaster in its own right. Darwin thought it might be heritable, but the qualities he had in mind—including John Stuart Mill's "energy and perseverance"—may not match up with our modern usage. We can certainly say that it's rare, though, and that it connotes startling originality, insight, and breadth. And it is by no means limited to the abstruse worlds of mathematics and science. Composers, artists, and writers are geniuses, too, so perhaps it has to do with finding or creating what wasn't there before—something, of course, worth finding.

As to picking out a list of twenty: "*quod homines tot sententiae*," said a sixteenth-century mathematician (about the right way to write out decimals), "as many opinions as there are people." Archimedes, Galileo, Newton, Darwin, and Einstein probably make everyone's scientific top twenty. Others included—or omitted—here may be more controversial. Nevertheless, each of these quirky, diverse individuals had that indefinable color of mind that finds nothing obvious about the obvious. To the modern world, some of their theorems and discoveries seem so matter-of-fact that we wonder why it took a genius to think of them. What matters here is context: how did each one grapple with these problems in his own time?

When Newton observed that he stood on the shoulders of giants, he said no more than the truth. Looking at the achievements of a few exceptional scientists and mathematicians helps focus history a bit. Even ivory-tower geniuses don't labor in intellectual isolation, spontaneously levering a world-view out of place overnight. In every case much of the work has already been done. Even the brilliantly wrong-headed—like Lamarck or Ptolemy—make first-rate puzzles. Perhaps in all fields, as in science, it takes a genius to figure out the answers, no matter who happened upon the questions.

Above: *The senate of Venice congregates for an astronomy lesson from Galileo and the thrill of looking through a telescope.*

Contents

Aristotle [384-322 BC]

Below: *A very Roman-looking Aristotle in the Palazzo Spada, Rome. The ancient Greek placed the highest value on setting out the rules of reasoning and organizing knowledge.*

Aristotle is known as the "father of modern science," yet his name has also acquired a sometimes unkind fame, associated with dusty and seemingly pointless mental chores. His mind was both large and subtle but he often tended toward mere list-making, and his premises are almost unfathomable to readers of later ages. How then, we may ask, did he ever manage to achieve a place in the history of science?

To overlook Aristotle is to miss the very beginnings of science, of a method that organizes nature in reasoned ways. His ordering of the natural world devolved from his much larger philosophical scheme of causes and forms and categories, which a modern scientist might find naive or even presumptuous. But the same might be said of successors to Newton who, at least briefly, beheld the cosmos as a grand piece of clockwork, a simple mechanism whose shafts and rotors were completely visible. Aristotle belongs in a world where the very notion of accounting reasonably for nature, of asking logically framed questions, was a novel starting place.

Student and Teacher of Great Minds

Born in Stagira, on the Macedonian coast, he was the son of Nicomachus, a court physician. At about the age of seventeen he went to Athens, where he studied with Plato for twenty years in that loosely constituted group known as the Academy (named after the public gymnasium where their gatherings took place). On the death of his great mentor, he began a period of wandering and teaching in Greece and its colonies, eventually being called back to Macedonia to instruct the heir to the throne, Alexander. After his student had conquered the known world, there was no place Aristotle couldn't go, but he chose Athens again, and there established his own lectures at the Lyceum. (A covered walk in its garden, the *peripatos*, gives his school of followers the name Peripatetics.) There he compiled the majority of his works that have survived. Earlier writings, some in the Academy's dialogue form, have disappeared. An insurrection following the death of Alexander in 323 BC convinced Aristotle of the prudence of moving along. He spent his last year on the island of Euboea.

The general format of Aristotle's works is very consistent. First he set up the parameters of the inquiry. He asked "what questions are we dealing with?" Then he defined his terms, outlining what his questions meant. There followed an extensive review of what others had thought on the subject, and a rapid dispatch of these ideas. Finally, he explained his own thinking in a strolling, though ordered style. An almost obsessive classifier, he strove for rules and method in every discipline, believing he should break his entire world into its progressively more fundamental parts and rebuild with a systematic method. Within the history of knowledge, he is remarkable not least for the sheer scope of his work, which addressed even collective wisdom and folk sayings.

In the *Physics*, Aristotle held that all science must proceed from the things that are known to the things that are less clear. He wrote three major treatises on biology, the *History of Animals, Parts of Animals, Generation of Animals*, and many minor ones. It's certain from these works that he must have dissected, vivisected, or had excellent reports of at least five hundred species. Aristotle is credited with originating classification by genus and species, more or less. He classified the life forms he studied in different ways; some seem familiar, others belong more narrowly to his time, his world, and his philosophy. He mentioned the importance of practical experimentation, but did not say *what* hypothesis was being tested or how.

"What is the nature of a thing?" was his biological question. Through his many observations he detected a vital force running through all life. Nature, for him, was a principle of movement or rest—living things contain that principle within them; they are vessels for nature, and pass the principle on to their offspring. These questions and answers seem today to have scant relevance to our understanding of biology.

Logic and Its Importance

Aristotle's next task was logic (or *organon*, meaning tool or instrument)—which he intended as the hammer of science. His famous cataloging of the forms of logical syllogism also continued his private vendetta against the Sophists, a rival philosophical tradition that displayed a tendency toward intellectual nihilism.

Of chief importance for his elucidation of logic were two principles: the *Law of Contradiction* and *the Law of the Excluded Middle*. The *Law of Contradiction* was a labor-saving device. It holds that a thing cannot both be and not be at the same time. Arguments could run on forever if reasonable people didn't accept this axiom. Several schools of thought denied the existence of any such imperative, namely the Heraclitean and Protagorean doctrines. Respectively, these can be summed up: "All is flux, nothing remains," and "Man is the measure of all things," or everything is relative. Aristotle took these challenges seriously—no discourse, scientific or otherwise, is possible within a framework that permits no general rules for what is valid reasoning and what is not.

Aristotle believed that no positive proof can be given for an axiom (this one no exception) but a preference can be expressed for its usefulness. He pointed out that nihilists could be refuted easily, if only they would oblige with any kind of positive statement about anything. He suspected them of simply posturing: "It is clear that no thinker, regardless of what school he may belong to, holds this view with any degree of sincerity." If everything is really everything else, he reasoned, then "why does he walk to Megara, and not stay at home…why does he not walk early one morning into a well or over the nearest precipice?"

The *Law of the Excluded Middle*, was another labor saver. It disallows any middle result between contradictories predicated of something. If all numbers are either even or odd, then there is no number which is neither—no number can fall within the excluded range between even and odd. This seems obvious but is still considered a problem by some; modern intuitionist mathematicians have built up multi-valued logics in which exclusive pairs of outcomes, like true/false or even/odd, do not exhaust the possibilities.

Aristotle believed in an ethical dimension to thought, that it wasn't just a plaything for sophists and wits.

Physics and Metaphysics

Physics, for Aristotle, was the study of nature, bearing little resemblance to the hard-nosed applied mathematics we know by the same name. His physics was teleological in kind, always fulfilling some discoverable purpose. He assumed, in other words, that everything is directed and fashioned toward some ultimate aim. His universe was made of four elements (earth, water, air, and fire) and brought about through four *causes*:

The *causes of matter and form* confer the limitations and structure of their components (the pot shatters by force, human flesh rots over time). The form or pattern of a thing further qualifies it (the ratio 2:1 is the specific formal cause of the octave in music). The *moving cause* is the agent that stops or starts any change in mutable things. The *final cause* is the most important cause of things in the world, the reason or purpose for which a thing exists.

A *potential*, or potency, the last major element in Aristotle's physics, is a principle of motion or change.

Not for several centuries would "physics" take on a more recognizable form.

In the *Metaphysics*, Aristotle discusses those things after (*meta*) physics, and specifically the essence of being. Every material thing has a cause—that's been covered in the *Physics*—but this chain is not infinite. Aristotle denied the existence of any infinities. Beyond the realm of the sensible is the world of substance, and behind that lies the prime mover. He deduced from the cycles of generation and destruction something operating, constant, good, always in the same way. At the heart of the universe, he imagined a perfect being, an absolute actuality that moves but is not moved.

Well, all of this was certainly one way of construing the world, though the answers toward which Aristotle toiled were to questions a modern mind would pose quite differently. His ideas were large enough though to hold academic attention for centuries. Even in Galileo's time, physicists were at work trying to discover the properties and tendencies of Aristotle's four elements or reasoning from first causes to solutions in mechanics. At its root, Aristotle's version of reality is too difficult and obscure for a quick appreciation. That he undertook a methodical examination of his world on such an epic scale, within such a consistent intellectual context, is a measure of his extraordinary genius.

Below: Plato, a mystic, poetic sort of philosopher walks with his more hardheaded student, Aristotle, in Raphael's "School of Athens."

The Infinity Quag

A crisis in Greek philosophical thought came about when discussion got around to the infinite. Mathematics was perfectly adorable so long as it made beautiful, rational music. Pythagoreans had a sense of knowing what their minds were for while contemplating the revealed truth of numbers. But infinity isn't revealed; or at least that kind of contemplation didn't feel right—it led nowhere. Everything that should unfold in divine order crumpled in contradictions. The cult of Pythagoras repressed infinity utterly.

A less fretful lot, the Stoics, actually enjoyed wrecking things with infinity—they supposed, more or less, that everyone would have to put up with a world in which nothing adds up to eternal sense, that trying to think oneself out of this irreducible condition is folly. The chief destroyer of intellectual comforts was Zeno of Elea (495–435 BC), who shocked Athens with four very famous paradoxes.

In the first (*Dichotomy*) he maintained motion is impossible. Whatever wishes to move from one place to another must first get halfway there, a quarter of the way before that, and so on, covering half of each interval before reaching any point or its path. But this means, right from the start, that there are an infinity of smaller and smaller distances needing to be covered before anything can budge; ergo, he reasoned, it can't be done.

The second puzzle, *Achilles*, restated the first in slightly different form. Here the goal line—a racing tortoise—is itself moving. Achilles tries to overtake the tortoise, but finds he must first reach all those positions—an infinity of them—the tortoise has already left behind. No matter how close he comes, Achilles always has more ground to make up.

Having proved that nothing starting from rest can ever really get moving, Zeno then shows that nothing which is moving can ever have been anywhere. In the third conundrum (the *Arrow*), an arrow in flight is always either at rest or not. That seems obvious. But if the arrow *is* moving, it can't be at a place for *any* measurable amount of time; if it were, it would be at rest, which it's not…and so the problem goes round in circles. It can all be dismissed blithely by contending that "the arrow occupies infinitely small places for infinitely small increments of time," but unless infinity is an engine that makes things move, the explanation bogs the arrow down in a multitude of resting places. The *Stadium*, the final paradox, has some overtaking and passing motion in it; a bit more complicated and less convincing.

Aristotle thought it important to throw out this dead-end attitude. It made everything seem, if not futile, somehow improvised. He allowed only "potential" infinities, never actual. But Zeno's thought-torture isn't so easily banished. Mathematicians still think about it, finding formal means of tiptoeing around infinitesimals, or meeting infinity head on, as Cantor did. Few have felt quite so comfortable as Aristotle about the problem.

Archimedes [ca. 287-212 BC]

Serious mathematics got off to a pretty fair start in the Western world with the work of several ancient Greeks and quite a few more of their successors in and around Alexandria. But progress stopped cold with the ascendancy of pragmatic Rome and the Arab destruction of the ancient world's greatest wonder, the Library at Alexandria, in AD 646. Over a million scrolls went up in flames. Math-

ematics remained dormant until, to name a date, 1246, the year in which an influential translation of Archimedes by William of Moerbeke appeared. For nearly six centuries the surviving texts, such as they were, had been held in the East, chiefly in Constantinople. The mathematician whom both Newton and Gauss would consider an equal, the creator of an integral calculus nearly two millennia ahead of the class, finally rejoined a living stream.

An Adventurous Spirit

Few facts about Archimedes' life have been preserved: a biography of the great mathematician by his friend Heracleides did not survive. Sporadic mentions by various classical authors establish that he was the son of an astronomer, Phidias, at Syracuse and probably related to that outlying city-state's ruler, King Hieron II. His famous discovery of the principle of buoyancy (which apparently came to Archimedes while stepping into the bathtub) is recorded as the solution to a problem posed by Hieron, who suspected an artisan of alloying the gold in his crown. By measuring the volumes of water displaced by the crown and an equal weight of gold—that is, comparing densities—the truth of the matter was revealed. Thus Archimedes enters history as the slightly distracted nemesis of consumer fraud.

When Syracuse was threatened by a Roman fleet, in 212 BC, Hieron prevailed upon Archimedes to oversee the city's defenses. Among the marvelous machines he is said to have thrown into the strategic balance were catapults hurling "Greek fire" (burning naphtha), giant grappling cranes—mounted on the seaward ramparts—and a large focusing mirror capable of igniting distant galleys. The mirror weapon sounds improbable, like a bit of

Hellenistic science fiction, yet Archimedes knew at least as much about parabolas as his contemporary Apollonius of Perga, who wrote *On Burning Glasses*, exploring the idea of concentration by another optical means. As to the galley-broaching machinery on the walls of Syracuse, an earlier account records that Archimedes tugged a loaded ship across the beach with an arrangement of compound pulleys. The grand old man of mechanical advantage, history remembers him for saying of levers that if he had but a place to stand, he could move the Earth.

Eventually, Marcellus, the Roman leader, took and sacked the city in an overland campaign waged from the rear. Legend has it that Archimedes was killed by a soldier while in rapt contemplation of a geometric diagram he'd traced in the sand. His grave was marked, as he had wished, with a chiseled slab depicting a sphere inscribed within a cylinder above the ratio of their volumes, 2:3. He thought it the most elegant of his many proofs (taste counted heavily in Greek mathematics).

Even as early as the fifth century BC, the adherents of Pythagoras were inclined to cast out anything that could not be expressed in integers. Euclideans, among others, promulgated the long-lived notion that geometry that can't be done with compass and ruler alone is merely expedient, an aesthetic cheat.

Almost everyone of his time, Archimedes included, found the useful application of mathematics a quotidian exercise, far removed from the true search for beauty—the beauty, that is, of pure mathematics. However, his tinkering with the practical possibilities suggested by his theorems proved remarkably productive. Aside from the kinds of engines present at the siege of Syracuse, he is generally credited with inventing a widely used irrigation device, the Archimedean screw or water snail, and ingenious model planetariums that displayed heavenly motions in their multiple courses and speeds. His treatises on water clocks, balances, and floating bodies seem to indicate, too, a thorough understanding of engineering.

Right: Though some-
what inefficient, the
Archimedean screw
draws water upward
with a useful mechanical
advantage. Simple and
durable, it saw service
around the Near East
for centuries.

Below: The area of a
parabolic segment
"exhausted" by filling its
interior with triangles
in ever closer approxi-
mations of the curve.
Finding areas of the
triangles is a simple
exercise. A series of area
sums for each new,
smaller group of trian-
gles approaches ever
closer to an implied final
value, just out of reach —
a limit, in modern
terminology.

New Proofs and Theorems

In matters of rigor and perfection, which is to say geometry, Archimedes deduced a great body of proofs concerning tangents, parallels, spirals, and giving the areas and volumes of elementary surfaces, the conic sections, and their solids of revolution. Among the theorems is an elegant trisection of the angle, but accomplished by sliding an element in its construction from one place to another—an illegal move in the tight little game of Greek compass-and-ruler geometry.

Methods of proof, as opposed to the rules of construction, had much greater range, a freedom to lift things off the table, as it were. One procedure, used and refined by Archimedes, entailed successively closer approximation to an implied endpoint, an "exhaustion" of the smaller and smaller differences between the assumed and the demonstrated. Curves, then, may be circumscribed or inscribed, or both, with polygons of known formula. The more sides, the more the polygon(s) comes to resemble the curve. And it may happen that successively better fits disclose a pattern, areas that appear to converge ever closer to some particular value—which is nowadays called a *limit*. (Proofs like this, with things vanishing

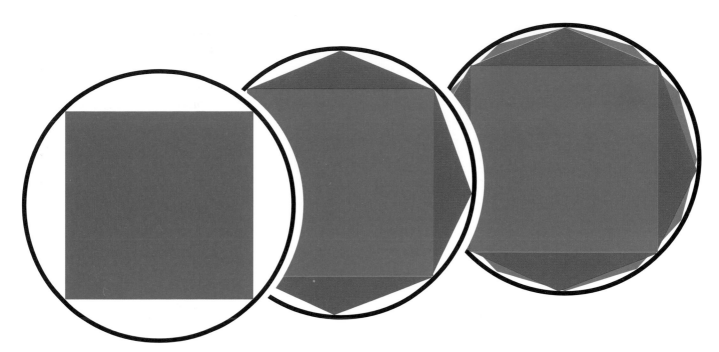

into infinitesimal differences, have come under heavy fire in the ultra-rigorous twentieth century, although mathematics seems in no danger of falling apart.) Thus, Archimedes sought the area under a parabola by first drawing a triangle within it. This triangle's area, obviously, is short of the parabola's area by the amount of the arclike leftovers that aren't covered. Now, if new, smaller triangles are drawn into the remaining spaces, leaving progressively less and less uncovered area within the parabola, the sum of their areas grows by ever smaller amounts toward a limiting value. (Each new "level" of triangle—first two of them, then four, and so on—is one sum.) The only trick, really, is to discern, or better yet, to deduce the pattern or rule by which the successive sums are growing—like showing that a series starting $\frac{1}{2} + \frac{1}{4} + \frac{1}{8} + \frac{1}{16}$ ... adds up to something infinitely close to 1 if you let it run long enough. In the parabola's case, the series of triangular sums progresses $1 + \frac{1}{4} + \frac{1}{4^2} + \frac{1}{4^3}$, and so on, pointing to a limit at $1\frac{1}{3}$ which, multiplied by the area of the first triangle, gives the area under the parabola. Except that it involves no mention of infinitesimals, the method amounts to a demonstration in

integral calculus. (He makes quite modern assumptions about series and infinite decomposition of surfaces and volumes in *On the Method of Mechanical Theorems*.)

The World in a Grain of Sand

Using the inside-outside method of exhaustion, Archimedes performed an impressive calculation of *pi*, approaching a circle from above and below and bracketing *pi* between $3\frac{1}{7}$ and $3\frac{10}{71}$. Even this degree of accuracy—it's about 0.2 percent off—required working off polygons of 96

Above and below: "Exhaustion" again, using polygons to approach the area of a circle (above). Below, a modern computer graphics display builds curves through a series of tiny, tangential segments.

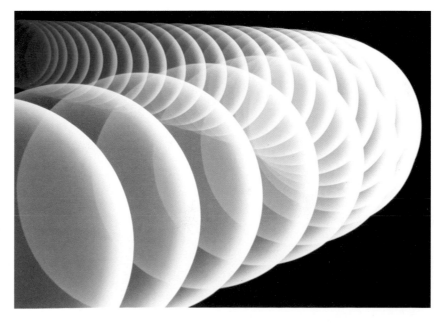

Right: One of the Seven Wonders of the Ancient World, the Pharos of Alexandria, an immense lighthouse reputedly 400 feet (122m) high. Its metal mirrors, ancient sources record, were designed by Archimedes. The light might have been seen as far as 30 miles (50km) away.

sides. (There exists no limiting value in this case, because *pi* is an *irrational*, expressible only as an unending, nonrepeating decimal.) What's so remarkable, really, is that he could do any intricate work at all with numbers, considering that the Greeks had not adopted any specialized system of numerals, nor a place-holding notation (a system in which, for example, digits indicating 100s precede those indicating 10s, which in turn precede those indicating single units). All the letters of the Greek alphabet did double duty as numbers. Greek math starts out, in effect, with a lot of grit in the wheels of computation. Of course, that only added more mystery to numbers, which wasn't displeasing to the philosopher-mathematicians. In any event, thinking about large numbers necessarily caused a good deal of churning in ancient Greek minds. Archimedes attended to certain problems of the number system in *The Sandreckoner:* he greatly improved, for himself at least, the notation and handling of numbers. His system contained a new unit, the

Right: At the siege of Syracuse, Archimedes is said to have ignited Roman galleys by focusing and directing sunlight with a parabolic mirror. Beyond actual manufacture, some practical difficulty lies in finding a galley that will linger for a time at the mirror's fixed focal distance.

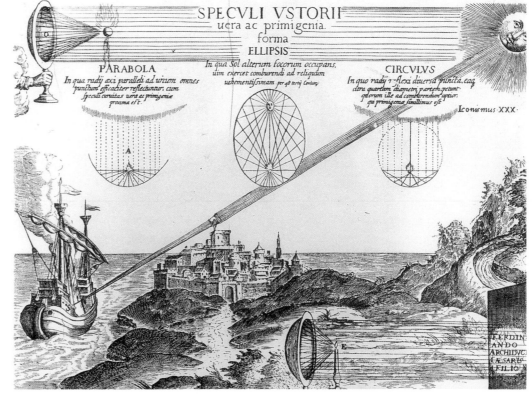

octade, which we would express as 100,000, and an exponential method of generating ever larger numbers from this base. It's a breakthrough in the cloudy quantitative thinking of his age, and he couldn't resist showing off a bit with a calculation of the number of grains of sand that would fill the universe. Postulating the diameter of the universe at 10,000 Earth diameters, and the Earth's diameter at 10,000 miles (300,000 Greek stadia), he comes up with 10^{63} grains of sand. He's wrong about everything, of course, except the power of his method. No one else had the slightest idea how to make numbers do these tricks; perusing *The Sandreckoner* may well have brought on sensations of dizziness and disorientation in its original readers.

That history should have held Archimedes' mathematical estate in probate for so long is not unusual; more puzzling is the fact that his style and results attracted few students in his own era. His works remained largely unknown in the Hellenistic and Roman worlds. It may be, as some scholars suggest, that he overreached the times. Pushing outward any further would seem to require both a new number symbolism and a willingness to embroil numbers with infinite magnitudes—a horror for any upright Greek mathematician, or any modern "intuitionist" for that matter. Fortunately, copies of his neglected works, or more often commentaries on them, reached Constantinople even as the Roman world order was disintegrating.

"The Master"

All available texts were compiled in the ninth century by Leon of Thessalonica in what has come down through history as "manuscript A." The collection contains all but four of the twenty or so surviving tracts. In his translation, Moerbeke had a copy of A to work with as well as a Manuscript B, which disappears from view sometime in the fourteenth century. It's a tantalizing story; though B remains lost,

a third Byzantine collation, Manuscript C, was discovered only in 1906 and brought the first look at *On Floating Bodies* since B had been misplaced. One piece, already cited, *On the Method of Mechanical Theorems*, was entirely new, previously known only by secondhand reference. Arab scholars, too, translated such fragments as came their way—Archimedes acquired great stature—but the collections are smaller, less definite in attribution and content.

If Archimedes had overreached his own culture, neither was Europe prepared for him in the twelfth century. The early, rather bad, translations were mired in scholastic interpretation, with endless splitting of hairs in the definition and classification of terms. At about the same time Moerbeke was finishing up his Archimedes, Thomas Aquinas was finalizing that warm union between scholastics and Aristotle. The migratory centuries don't end for Archimedes until the Renaissance, when his ideas fell out of suspension so naturally that it were as if no time at all had passed. The Greek, "the Master" as he was known to Arab admirers, would have been at ease conversing with Newton, Euler, or Gauss.

Above: *Too busy working through problems to notice the entry of Roman conquerors, Archimedes was killed when he ordered a soldier to step out of his light.*

The Geometers

Below: *Euclid set the paradigmatic form of mathematical rigor in his immortal* Elements of Geometry.

N o one can be certain how much of Greek mathematics was lost in the ashes of the Great Library at Alexandria, which once housed a fabulous cultural wealth. From other sources, of course, many major works have been recovered or partially reconstructed; we can hope with some confidence that our picture is reasonably whole.

Archimedes belonged to an especially bright generation of mathematicians, roughly including Aristarchus, Euclid, Eratosthenes, Apollonius, and such lesser lights as Autolycus, Aristaeus, and Eudemus. Before them, in the fourth century BC, had come Eudoxus, perhaps the first mathematician we might recognize as having the necessary equipment for the job. Once a protegé of Plato—who wasn't much of a mathematician—Eudoxus settled finally in Ionia, at Cnidus, where he occupied himself as a physician and astronomer when he wasn't doing math. He is credited with the method of exhaustion and the earliest general solutions for curved lines, areas, and volumes. It is said that the theorems of Eudoxus inspired Euclid to gather up and organize the best of Greek geometry into the immortal *Elements*, both the glory and the bane of deductive method.

Regrettably, Eudoxus also bequeathed a conception of the universe in concentric transparent spheres of which ecclesiastical authorities grew enamored in a later age. Dislodging the error cost some suffering for Galileo, among others, when it came time to separate dogma from gravitational acceleration. Eudoxus, for one, wouldn't have persisted in the face of better observational explanations. The cosmos was open in his time to a looser set of conjectures. Aristarchus, reasoning from such evident facts as the larger size of the sun compared with the Earth, had the planet orbiting a stationary sun.

Apollonius, the purest intellect of the group, was deeply immersed in geometry. His discoveries, which fathom the prop-

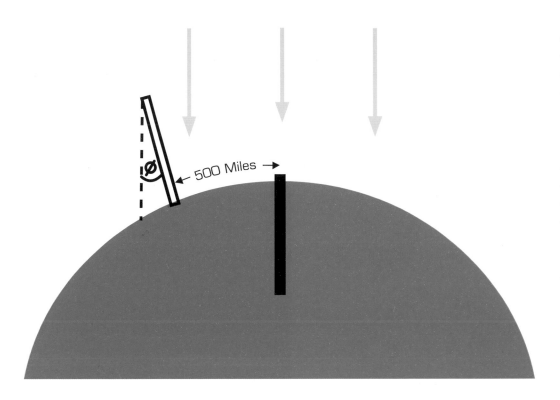

500 Miles

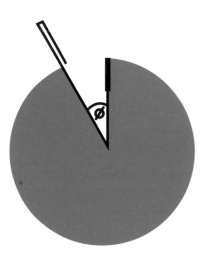

Left: *Eratosthenes'
calculation of Earth's
circumference depends
crucially on the angle of
the shadow (about 7.5°)
cast at Alexandria while
the sun is directly over-
head at Syene. It must,
by Euclidean reckoning,
be the same as the angle
at Earth's center of the
intersection of Earth's
radii drawn from Syene
and Alexandria. With
the distance between the
cities known, the plane-
tary girth is given by
multiplying by* $^{360}/_{7.5}$*,
the number of segments
needed to go round the
whole circle.*

erties of conic sections, are the summit of Greek geometry. His equal isn't seen again until the seventeenth century. But it's Eratosthenes who captures the imagination: he contrived to measure the size of the Earth! To do so, he arranged that the midday shadow of a tall tower in Alexandria be measured on the same day of the year in which the midday sun could be seen, briefly, reflected from the bottom of a well at Syene, 500 miles distant. Since the sun on that day stood, obviously, directly overhead in Syene, its slight angle from the vertical as seen from Alexandria—due to the curvature of Earth's surface—can be used to calculate the number of 500-mile segments in one full span of the Earth. Eratosthenes figured a circumference of about 24,000 miles, which is only a thousand miles or so too small (less than 4 percent error), though later geographers tended to believe the result far too large. If Columbus had known what Eratosthenes knew, who's to say he would have had the same enthusiasm for a voyage westward?

19

Galileo Galilei (1564-1642)

Below: Galileo Galilei, a preeminent scientist in an age given to wordy, philosophical dispute, opened up the heavens through telescopic observation. Modern physics began with his insistence on experiment and mathematical interpretation.

Galileo has taken rather a battering in the popular history of science: an eccentric man dropping cannonballs off the Leaning Tower of Pisa, perhaps inventing a telescope next afternoon, then falling straight away into the clutches of the Inquisition—something about the Earth going around the sun. There isn't much plot to the schoolboy version. The truth, naturally, is somewhat subtler and richer.

Gravity Before Newton

The Leaning Tower myth may have originated with a genuine, albeit crude attempt to challenge Aristotelian gravity theory. The Dutch scientist, Simon Stevinus, had done such an experiment a few decades before Galileo began to consider the problem. (Stevinus, by the way, popularized the use of decimal fractions in European mathematics.) The idea was to show that things fall at the same rate regardless of weight and size. Such imprecise dabbling in the effects of gravity had led to many pointless disputations as to what was really going on. Everyone with academic standing had the impression that things speed up when you let go of them, that they continued falling at a more or less constant velocity, and that the size of the objects might or might not count in the result. Scientifically speaking, the late sixteenth century had a keen curiosity and a tendency to bog down in a hypothetical morass. The way out, as Galileo and very few others realized, is experiment, observation, and mathematics.

The son of a successful musician, Galileo was intended by his father for the best that late Renaissance education could bestow, a "profession." Until recent centuries, that always meant law, theology, or medicine. Galileo enrolled, thus, in 1581 to study medicine at the University of Pisa. Though he followed the curriculum for four years, he left without his degree. He'd become distracted by exposure to such speculative topics as mathematics and "natural philosophy," a portmanteau course chiefly composed of declamations of the ancients on how and what the physical world ought to be, even if it weren't. Happily, Galileo was able to eke out his studies with a year of study under the mathematician Ostilio Ricci at the Florentine court.

Considering himself (rightly) as prepared as anyone in northern Italy to teach the subject, Galileo offered mathematical lectures in Siena, Florence, and finally at the University of Pisa, beginning in 1589. As he must have known, Pisa was a dead end, hidebound in Aristotelian philosophizing and proud of it. Embroiling oneself in controversies over how things partake of essence and why things float (Aristotle said shape, but Galileo knew better) could only sap a sharp intellect. By 1592 he had achieved an invitation to instruct in mathematics at the University of Padua, a position he held for the next eighteen years. Not only did his pay and the esteem for his work grow substantially, but Padua fell within the Venetian Republic, which put it effectively beyond the meddling and intrigues of Church and ducal courts.

At Padua in 1604, Galileo finally settled for himself how objects behave in falling. The experiment was classic, quite as illuminating within its context as any critical quantum result of our present era. To begin, he redirected the forces in the problem: vertical drops exceeded good experimental means; for one thing, precision timekeeping didn't go much beyond counting off pulsebeats. His masses were made to roll through a greater distance, and time, down gently sloped wooden channels. He kept track with a water clock of his own devising. Galileo correctly perceived that gravity must continue to act proportionately to the ramp's height. Furthermore, he well understood that physical experiments merely approach ideals; he reports a hundred trials at various settings. His own word for "experiment," by the way, was *cimento*, "ordeal"; science may have lost a brooding nuance.

Galileo noted that unequal masses fall in equal times. And because he was an able mathematician, he noted that distance intervals increase by law of the square against elapsed time, which could only

mean to him a constant acceleration at work. This does not mean he had discovered the law of gravity, but he had certainly set out what kind of law it must be. Two generations later, Newton and Christian Huygens found in Galileo the starting point for their own investigations. Neither is the finding of equal acceleration for unequal masses a trivial one. Quite modern and serious-minded physicists (Eötvos and Lorand in the late nineteenth century, Braginsky and Dicke more recently) continued to work at finding the limits, if there are any, within which this property of mass and gravity is true.

Above: In the cathedral of Pisa, the young Galileo musing on the regular swaying of a suspended lamp. Some years later, he was ready to express the equal times elapsed with each swing as a general law of pendulums (isochronicity)— though he didn't make plans for a working timekeeper until nearly the end of his life.

Above: *Nicholas Copernicus (1473–1543) reasoned from astronomical observations that the planets must revolve around a stationary sun.*

Opposite: *Posing allegorically with Urania, the muse of astronomy, are luminaries including Ptolemy, Copernicus, and Galileo (with pointer).*

to ballistics were obvious. There are actually two tricks, one that we usually take for granted. Galileo had satisfied himself that the horizontal component (neglecting friction) remains constant, that a body in motion continues in that state until acted upon by some external force. He assumed, in other words, Newton's first law of motion, a concept resisted by his contemporaries.

A Free Thinker

What's perhaps most refreshing about Galileo, and rare enough in any era, is the free detachment of his judgment from doctrine. Any position contradicted by results is a position worth abandoning, or at least re-examining. His correspondence confides that he had held opinions on the unlikelihood of constant acceleration in gravity, but his view was progressively modified with each new experiment. Once, to Kepler, he wrote that he could conceive natural, mechanical explanations for all natural phenomena save for the tides. Yet he never ceased applying his ingenuity to the problem. (No demonstrable means of tying the moon into the picture existed before Newton.) Eventually he did arrive at a sort of "slosh" solution arising out of Earth's accelerations in orbit and resultant radial velocities in sea water at different latitudes. Anyone who hasn't a feel for the breadth, subtlety and elegance of Galileo's thinking should try working through this proposition. That the moon accounts for tides we now know, but could there be a "slosh" effect nonetheless? Physicists armed with the tools of analysis and more perfected theory remained intrigued by the idea until the late nineteenth century, when the great Ernst Mach finally pronounced it unworkable. With genius, the mistakes can be as interesting as the successes. (Galileo may have been the only man in Europe to have concluded that comets were optical illusions.)

Over the years Galileo's ranging mind continued to transform the disorder of experience into numbers, often enough with practical results. His discovery and correct formulation of the isochronicity of pendulums (*i.e.*, the equal times of each swing) led to new means of timekeeping. He actually got around to a consideration of such devices in the last year of his life, but it was left to Huygens to build a working model. He was first, as well, to describe precisely the paths, parabolas, traced by moving objects while falling. The trick involves decomposing motion into horizontal (constant) and vertical (accelerated) components. Applications

Right and below right:
*From among Galileo's
many careful drawings
as he sat at his telescope:
Saturn's rings (right),
and Earth's moon pocked
with craters.*

*Below: Two telescopes
built by Galileo. His
best—with lenses he
ground himself—
magnified by a factor of
approximately thirty and
was strong enough to
shake entrenched dogma.*

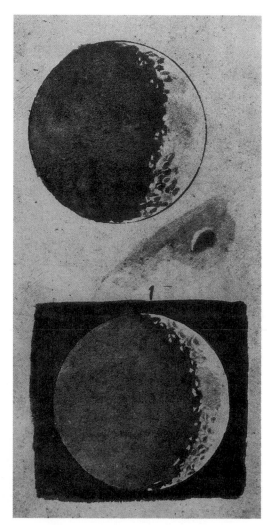

Apparently, Galileo had not embraced the Copernican view that planets orbit the sun before 1597. Certainly Tycho Brahe, Europe's leading astronomer, would never accept the notion. Observation, however, forced a change of mind for Galileo. And by 1610 he had the world's best telescopes—built by himself—to confirm and explore the truth. Here, of course, is where trouble with the Church began, but this part of the story, too, is a good deal more complex than the usual historical gloss.

The Vatican Machine

The sixteenth-century Roman Catholic Church was the largest functioning institution in Europe and probably the best organized. Its various departments, bureaus, "offices," kept up with events everywhere, including developments in science. Christopher Clavius, chief Jesuit astronomer and a correspondent with Galileo, had looked through Galileo's new telescopes—a number of clerics, predictably, would not—and drawn the right conclusions from what he saw. No enlightened cleric doubted that new instructions would have to be worked out.

Within the sophisticated ecclesiastical ambit of Rome, at levels of high Church policy, there was little objection to the Copernican view. If certain rustic friars insisted, per the Bible, that Joshua saw the sun stopped in the heavens (thus it must orbit Earth), it needn't trouble those who speculated about an immobile sun at the center of a family of orbiting planets. To maintain a thing theologically was a doctrinal act, not at all the same as to adopt positions in the spirit of philosophical discourse. Even where hemmed in by emerging knowledge or

other apparent conflict between reason and faith, the Church might always discover a divine illusion at work—or appeal to the Jesuits for more convincing arguments. The Church had, after all, completely absorbed most of Greek philosophy without leaving many lumps in the dogma. Long before the time of Copernicus, the Church had known the heliocentric theory as Pythagorean, a harmless enough object of contemplation, even a little mathematical, like admiring Euclidean theorems. No one really yet suspected how much damage mere mathematics could do in the *real* world.

at once: there were moons around Jupiter, valleys and mountains in Earth's moon, spots on the sun, a *rotating* sun, stars in the Milky Way. Of course, by 1609 Kepler had already published two of his three laws of planetary orbital motion; it simply hadn't the impact of what was visible through the

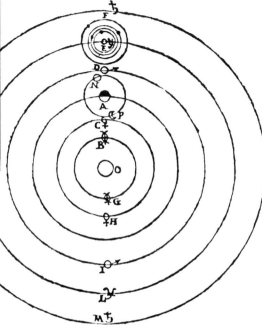

Galileo communicated the discoveries made with his new telescopes in 1610 in *Nuncius Siderius* (usually translated *The Starry Messenger*) and in frequent notes over the next few years. The polished orbs and celestial spheres of geocentric Ptolemaic cosmology all shattered

Left: Copernicus and his new solar system: moons orbiting the planets, and planets turning round the sun—depicted with circular paths. Kepler would divine the true, elliptical courses of orbiting bodies.

Below: The senate of Venice congregates for an astronomy lesson from Galileo and the thrill of looking through a telescope.

Top: In Rome, an aged Galileo defends himself before the Inquisition in a trial fraught with irregularities and mislaid documents.

Above: John Milton, the great English poet, was among Galileo's distinguished visitors during his permanent confinement at his home in Arcetri.

cial sense, that his views could not be defended or held—an admonishment, in effect, to make less noise. And here the Church's institutional politics took over the story and the fate of Galileo.

No sooner had the session concluded than a dissatisfied faction let it be known that Galileo had been made to recant, that his views constituted heresy. As subsequent proceedings (in 1633) were to show, the official record of the session with Bellarmine had disappeared. Bellarmine went to the trouble of issuing a clarification three months after the meeting, but to little effect. For his part, Galileo kept an eight-year public silence on the subject of Earth's place in the universe.

When the scientifically inclined Maffeo Barberini, an admirer of Galileo, became Pope Urban VIII in 1623, he pronounced the Copernican system rash but not heretical. His announcement had no settling effect on the turmoil in the ranks. Cabals formed and broke on this and other issues (Europe had just embarked on its last and bloodiest politico-religious struggle, the Thirty Years War), and the Jesuits were finally thrown into the balance against Galileo. Matters came to a head in 1632 with Galileo's publication of *Dialogue on the Two Chief World Systems.*

Since the election of Urban VIII, Galileo had cautiously resumed public discourse and, perhaps underestimating his enemies in Rome, had ventured to submit his manuscript to the Inquisitor at Florence for clearance to publish. In fact, the book passed Church scrutiny and had its official license to go to press. The aftermath is a sorry episode for the Church: the aging, arthritic Galileo was brought up before the Inquisition, found guilty of violating his abjuration of 1616—no other charge could succeed because of the lack of documentation—and confined under house arrest at Arcetri for the remainder of his life. His works remained on the Index (of proscribed books) until 1822. In confinement, Galileo

lenses. When the jolt hit the working theocracy—priests and friars—the reactionary commotion percolated quickly to the top, resulting in a convocation of Qualifiers (experts) of the Holy Office in 1616. That body came down firmly on the side of a stationary Earth, as doctrine required.

Galileo, meanwhile, had capitalized on his growing repute and accepted in 1610 an appointment in Florence to the Grand Duke of Tuscany, once again within political hailing distance of the Vatican. He was summoned to an audience in Rome with Cardinal Bellarmine soon after the Qualifiers reported their findings. In a cordial encounter Galileo agreed, in an offi-

Left: A modern radio telescope continues, with conspicuously improved technology, the Galilean tradition of methodical observation.

Below, left: Today, with cameras actually orbiting the moon, its topography is known as completely as any earthly mountain range and better than some regions of the ocean floor.

stayed vigorous in mind, turning out his most important treatment of mechanics, *Discourses Upon Two New Sciences*, and receiving distinguished admirers including Thomas Hobbes, John Milton, and the Italian physicist Evangelista Torricelli.

Galileo Today

Even with his death, the books never really closed: clerical sleuths, on the one hand, continue to sift the archives for a clearer picture of the trial, while astronomers keep turning the pages of his notebooks. In fact, Galileo is still posing problems in celestial mechanics. In 1980, with new appreciation for the accuracy of his observational methods, researchers discovered that Galileo plotted positions of Neptune during the years 1612 and 1613. Galileo did not realize that he was looking at another planet—Johann Galle made that discovery in 1846—but the positions he marked out, if correct, conflict disturbingly with modern computations of Neptune's assumed whereabouts in 1612–13. Neptune's 165- year orbit may be distorted by influences, other masses in the solar system, not yet accounted for in the equations: the planet hasn't completed even a full turn since the time of its discovery.

Below: Long-voyaging imaging technology reveals the planets in ever greater detail: here, the stormy vortex of a gigantic red spot on Jupiter, four of whose satellites Galileo discovered in 1610.

Elliptical Thinking

DIALOGVS DE SYSTEMATE MVNDI,
Autore
GALILÆO GALILÆI LYNCEO,
SERENISSIMO
FERDINANDO II. HETRVR. MAGNO-DVCI
dicatus.

ARISTOT. CL. PTOLEM. N. COPERNICVS.

Augustæ Treboc.
Anno S. Impensis BONAVENTVRÆ et ABRAHAMI ELZEVIR. 1635
Bibliopolar. Leydens.

Above: *Frontispiece of* The System of Two Worlds, *the book that got Galileo into trouble. Kepler had accepted the Copernican view earlier than Galileo.*

Right: *A medieval astronomer taking navigational measurements.*

sumably because the notion of elliptical orbits wasn't much to Galileo's taste—and Kepler's style taxes even patient readers. Kepler served five years as Tycho Brahe's assistant; he inherited the great astronomer's notebooks. From these and his own observations, Kepler reached three rather epochal conclusions: first, planets orbit in elliptical, not circular, paths around a sun occupying one focus of each ellipse; second, as measured by some imaginary arm from sun to planet, a planet sweeps out equal areas within the ellipse in equal times; third, cubes of average planetary distances from the sun are proportional to squares of the times it takes to complete an orbit. Creditable mathematics all around—one would never suspect Kepler was more concerned with reducing the cosmos to something like musical notation than merely with plotting orbital tracks. (He'd actually deduced a few of the planetary tunes by the time Book Five of his *Harmony of the World* appeared.)

The seventeenth century's new generation of physicists included one particularly odd fellow, Johannes Kepler. His biographers are apt to cringe when describing his bizarre turns of mind, though time and again he did somehow arrive at perfectly true results from quite absurd premises. "Sleepwalker" is a term not infrequently heard. Although Galileo valued his friendship, he nonetheless left Kepler's *De Revolutionibus* unread for many years, pre-

What was wrong with Kepler's work? Probably too much mathematics, too much Aristotle, and an ungovernable mysticism. Kepler seems to have swallowed whole the works of the Greeks. To Aristotle's natural and reasonable ordering of things, Kepler fused Pythagorean mysticism, all summed up for him in the search for sublime harmonies in nature. In the mathematical scheme of things, this necessarily leads to an exhausting regimen. The prevailing cosmology before Kepler's time was that of the second-century Alexandrian Claudius Ptolemy.

Whereas Aristotle had passed along (from Eudoxus) a universe of frictionless crystal spheres turning within one another, Earth immobile at the center, Ptolemy had found it necessary to complicate the scheme if the apparently recessional motions of the planets were to be explained. Good results dictate such measures as shifting the centers of various spheres and having some smaller ones actually rolling around inside others. (Points on the surface of such a captive orb describe graceful loops, called epicycloids.) With this cumbersome mechanics even the most complex curves might be approximated, but at the cost of tremendous computational and conceptual labor. No one ever called the Ptolemaic universe simple-minded. From the time of Newton, better analytical methods (the calculus) came into use, clearing away much of the clutter.

Kepler, trying to fit a celestial system around Brahe's observations, didn't adopt the Copernican (heliocentric) view until years of effort with tortured epicycloids failed to produce a believable model. Of course, being Kepler, he was simultaneously attempting to derive orbits in terms of the five regular geometric solids and demonstrate, as well, "that the four kinds of voice are expressed in the planets: soprano, alto, tenor, and bass." Certainly, he'd set himself a program worthy of genius, though probably not one achievable within the realm of physics.

Above: *Johannes Kepler, whose thinking combined the mathematical with the mystical. His sublime visions never quite matched the observable heavens.*

Left: *Musical motifs, "music of the spheres," associated by Kepler with the various planets—the scale derivable, he believed, from the orbital speeds.*

William Harvey [1578-1657]

Few would choose today to debate the workings of, say, the cardiovascular system as a matter of philosophical inquiry. In this, at least, the seventeenth century arranged such medical knowledge as it possessed within a very different framework than might a modern scientist. The usual benchmark for the soundness of one's views was, of course, Aristotle. Physicists had begun jumping ship somewhat earlier than physicians, since the kinds of

Gulielmus (Magnus ille) Harveus

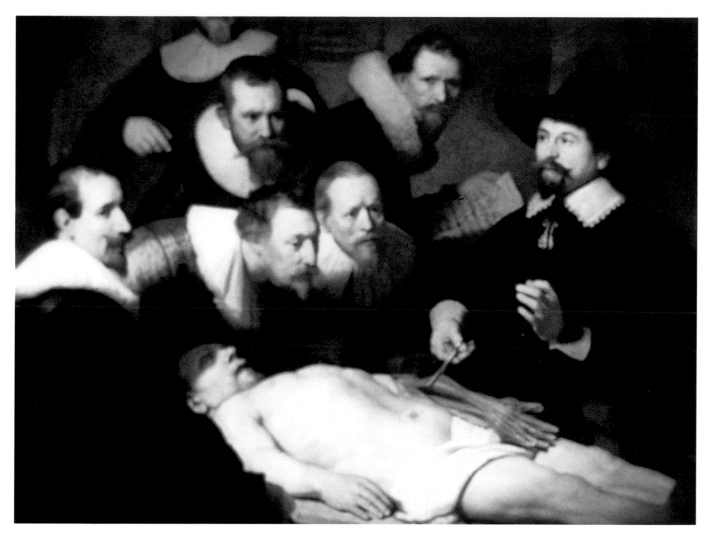

problems run into by the mathematical types were not usually stuff of dogma. But if a medical problem is reduced at the outset to terms asking where the essence of life, or soul, or generative spirit resides within the body, then anatomy becomes just another sort of uplifting reading.

The Heart of the Matter

It's not that the anatomists did sloppy work, but that human bodies don't come apart in mechanistic fragments like the orbits of planetary satellites. When William Harvey, the very best of his generation, had correctly described the heart's action and irrefutably shown how it gives rise to circulation of the blood, he still hadn't found the purpose. It's one thing to know that blood is pumped through the body, quite another to know why. This

redounds to his credit as a scientist, for his methods of observation were so scrupulous that he had to insist upon his findings no matter how they might fit into a veiled larger picture.

Harvey, the son of affluent English parents, attended medical classes at the University of Padua, the leading institution in the field, from 1599 to 1602. (The dates might have brought him into contact with one of Padua's newer professors, Galileo Galilei, but there is no evidence that they met.) In those years at Padua, the doctrinal lines in medicine descended through either Aristotle or Galen. The anatomist Fabrici generally supported Galen; the philosopher Cremonini, Aristotle. Inasmuch as Galen had a lot of first-hand experience with human anatomy—he'd patched up gladiators in

Above: In a famous painting by Rembrandt, The Anatomy Lesson, *the rather formal nature of such demonstrations is apparent. Until Harvey's time, most dissections served as perfunctory affirmations of the ancients, Aristotle and Galen.*

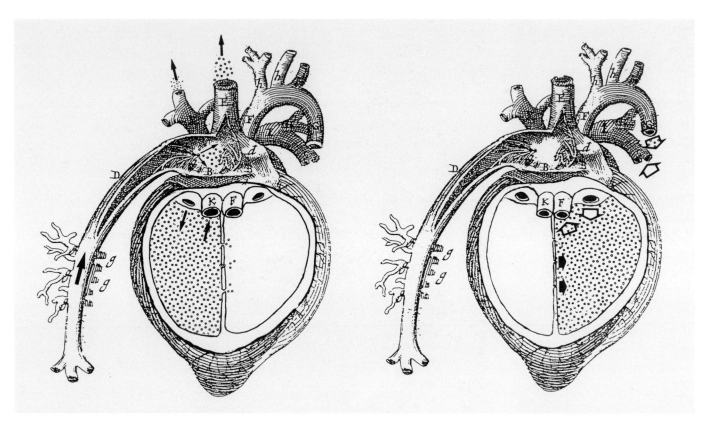

Above: *Action of the heart according to Galen: the left side chiefly concerned with moving blood from liver to lungs; the right side mostly transporting air, but mixed with blood seeping across the heart's dividing septum. Galen's heart forcibly expanded with each pulse beat, instead of contracting, and was believed to draw blood to itself rather than muscularly expelling it.*

Rome—practitioners tended to prefer Galen's views in physiology. The systematic inferences of Aristotle appealed more to academic philosophers. Harvey himself found Aristotle, on the whole, a meaningful guide, but he never undertook experiments merely to fit in with a grander scheme.

Of course, it might be pointed out that doctors of that day had little enough to occupy them professionally; all that they had to work with was a limited supply of cadavers, the books, and the disputes. The routine of medicine consisted largely in making diagnoses of imbalances in the bodily fluids (the four "humors") and prescribing foul concoctions, bloodletting, and a change of air. Surgery, a much inferior calling, was left to dubiously qualified but strong-armed practitioners. Only in the mid-sixteenth century, through the influence of Andreas Vesalius, had anatomical curricula begun to employ dissection as more than a ritual demonstration.

After graduating and returning to London, Harvey applied himself ener-

getically to his discipline, gaining appointment to St. Bartholomew's Hospital, conducting anatomical researches, reforming instruction, and eventually delivering lectures of notable freshness and vivacity. He married well, a connection that aided his appointment, in 1619, as physician to King James I. Upon the succession of Charles I, he remained at court in the same capacity. His association with the House of Stuart cost history dearly; in the turmoil of the Civil War (1642–48) he removed with the king to Oxford. A great many of the loyal doctor's notes and papers were wantonly destroyed in the sack of his quarters by Parliamentary troops. More perished in the Great Fire of 1666. Financially ruined as well, Harvey spent his last decade staying by turns with friends and with his many brothers, all of them merchants. Although handled roughly by the times, he was still independent of mind and revered by his colleagues when he died in 1657.

To understand the profound impression made by Harvey's chief discovery, the circulation of the blood, it's helpful to see the problem as it appeared to a top-notch seventeenth-century intellect. First, attention centered, as it had from Aristotle's day, on the blood: What is it? What's it doing in the body? Harvey concluded after long study that it is the very stuff of life. Here he followed Aristotle to the extent that he considered life an intrinsic quality of bodily tissue and not something somehow added to it, or temporarily resident within it. Other theorists, notably Galen, had argued for various interactive schemes that ascribed to shapes or arrangements of the organs a large share in bringing life about.

The organs caused difficulty for everyone. They seemed mere auxiliaries to life in Harvey's view, their function uncertain. Galenists got no further; they simply spread the problem out over a larger area. Whatever its purpose though, the inces-

sant motion of the heart held everyone's attention. Aristotle had likened it to a "separate animal." If the heart could be explained, prevailing reason went, some of the big questions would be settled. The anatomist Colombo had maintained, in 1559, that blood reached one side of the heart from the other only by passing through the lungs, but that only brought in another organ whose function was problematic—perhaps cooling the blood, or getting rid of the body's vapors. The fact that blood in different vessels had very different colors (bright red in arteries, darker and brownish in veins) convinced Galen and most later anatomists that there were two or three different bloodlike substances.

With the success of mechanical explanations in physics, medical theorists began to wonder about the heart as an engine: maybe it heated the blood. But it had usu-

Below: Demonstrating circulation of the blood to Charles I. Harvey was both physician and friend to this very healthy monarch—circumstances that granted Harvey time for teaching and research. The royal connection was to result, though, in the senseless destruction of much of Harvey's work by Cromwell's troops.

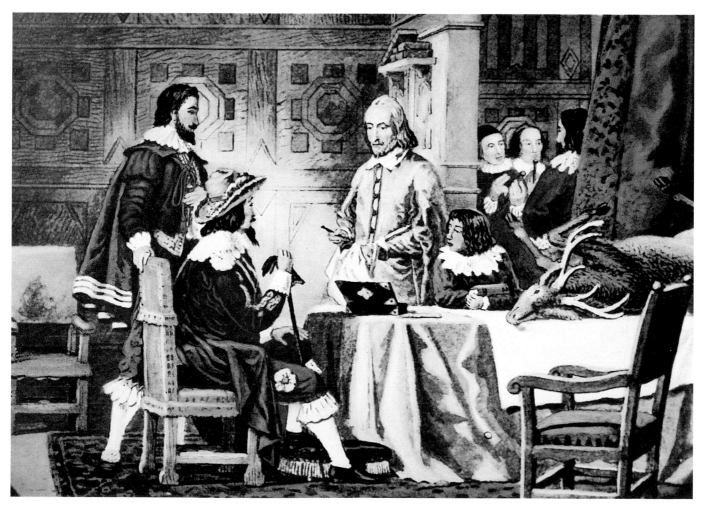

Below: Ingenious
demonstrations provided
evidence for blood
circulation—here an
arm has been tied to
obstruct blood flow,
while weakened pulse
beats are detected at
pressure points.

ally been assumed that blood somehow did its own heating—part of the mysterious life-force. Fabrici, Harvey's teacher, had already discovered valves in the veins. He reasoned that they kept blood from accumulating in the extremities. Harvey, by no means alone, believed the large valves in the heart itself wouldn't be there unless they served a purpose.

The Evidence for Circulation

It may seem today that, with so many clues available, the world was dawdling over drawing the right conclusions. Not for many decades, however, would circulation make much sense to scientists. No one had the faintest chemical idea about the body's energy mechanisms, what sort of basic functions it must carry out, or even that oxygen existed.

Harvey, a superb scientist in his pursuit of the right questions, discovered circula-

tion only because he perceived the direction in which experiments must go if diverse observations were to be resolved. He published the fruits of his investigation in 1628 in *De Motu Cordis* (its full title is an exercise in Latin).

In a coherent series of experiments, some as simple as applying tourniquets, Harvey tested manifestations of flow. Working with snakes, he denied blood to areas of the heart and noted the effects of removing constriction. He related his findings to anatomical structures and to such well-known phenomena as the rapid spread of a toxin through the bloodstream. Together, the results confirmed circulation as the sole consistent explanation. Further, he established that the heart's action is that of a pump, expelling blood in the contractile part of its cycle, the systole. The last link in his chain of proof, the capillaries, he was unable to

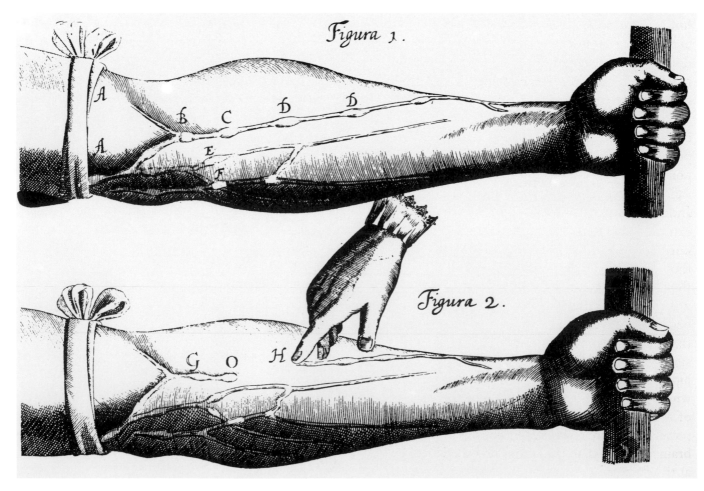

find—there were no microscopes—but on the strength of his evidence, few doubted that time would bear out the hypothesis. (Marcello Malpighi made that discovery in 1661.)

True, until the end of his life Harvey could not satisfy himself as to the purpose of the blood's circulation, but he pointed out to critics that this was not a valid reason to reject a demonstrated fact. Indeed, most of the scientific world exulted in the new impetus to medical knowledge. Harvey's work continued, though little enough of it came through the Civil War and the Great Fire. In an unfinished treatise, "On Locomotion," begun in 1627, he had already realized that nerves "communicate something sensible [sensations] to the brain so that a judgment can be made." Of the brain, he wrote that it orchestrated the movements of the muscles but did not supply the power. These are much clearer notions of brain function than those that prevailed at the time.

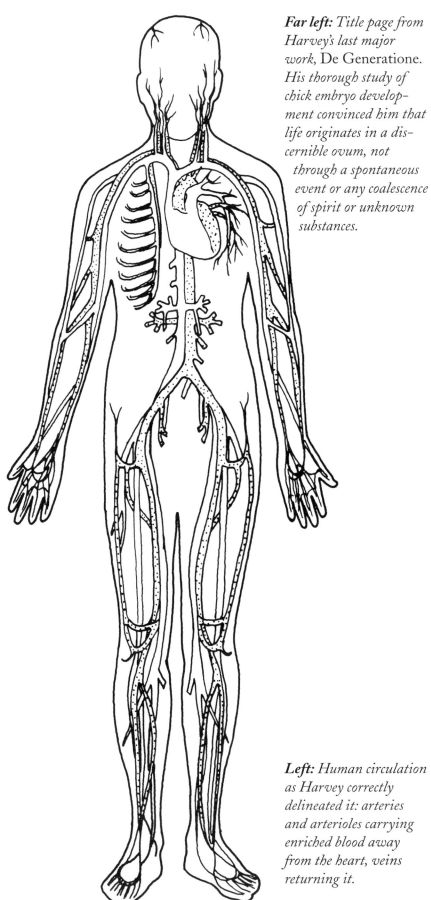

Far left: Title page from Harvey's last major work, De Generatione. *His thorough study of chick embryo development convinced him that life originates in a discernible ovum, not through a spontaneous event or any coalescence of spirit or unknown substances.*

Left: Human circulation as Harvey correctly delineated it: arteries and arterioles carrying enriched blood away from the heart, veins returning it.

The Errant Lore of Medicine

Right: *Galen (AD 131– 201), a Greek physician of the Roman era, attended gladiators and emperors, and made his fortune as well as a legend of himself. His observations weren't improved upon significantly for about fourteen centuries.*

Below: *The quack seems to thrive in every time and place, as in this unnecessary bloodletting rendered by Hieronymous Bosch.*

That any of the tradition of Greek or Roman medicine was passed along in the western world is due largely to Islamic scholarship and a few libraries left intact within conquered Islamic territory. Two philosopher-physicians in particular, Avicenna and Averroes, left commentaries that were translated into Latin and circulated widely. Avicenna (or Ibn-Sina, 980–1037), a Persian, transmitted through his encyclopedic manuscripts chiefly the learning of Galen, which was in turn influenced by Hippocrates and Aristotle. He left behind, as well, seven treatises on the alchemical philosopher's stone and a reputation for hedonistic dissipation that has followed him through history. In Moorish Spain, Averroes (Abdul-Ibn-Rushd, 1126–1198) enlarged principally on the texts of Aristotle, unknown in Europe through most of the Middle Ages.

Inasmuch as medical treatment remained a harrowing practice through the nineteenth century, it may fairly be surmised that recovering the ancient texts didn't do much for its development. Getting back to Greek basics like the four "humors"—blood, phlegm, yellow bile, and black bile—promoted long discussions of temperament, disharmony, and the like, but with no advances other than in academic distinction. On the other hand, the new mainstream medicine probably killed patients no more frequently than more patently superstitious, folkloric regimes.

Notable iconoclasts appeared among the legions of pretenders, sometimes promoting treatments of some use. The greatest of all the quacks, Aureolus Theophrastus Bombastus von Hohenheim, a.k.a. Paracelsus (1493–1541), publicly burned the works of Avicenna and Galen to inaugurate his lectures at the University of Basle. He also maintained he kept up a correspondence with Galen from hell, so there must have been one or two points yet unsettled between them. A showman and brawler, immersed in astrology and alchemy, Paracelsus possessed a practical style, trying out compounds of sulfur, copper, iron, lead, and mercury on his patients. His therapeutic use of opium, at any rate, must have alleviated many symptoms.

The most incisive and dedicated of Harvey's forerunners is undoubtedly Ambroise Paré (1517–1590), a man quite literally up from the ranks in medicine. He'd served at the bottom, as a barber's apprentice, and later as a French regimental surgeon. Eventually, he was appointed to a quick succession of five French kings (bad joust, sickly child, dynastic assassination—Paré should not be judged on actuarial appearances). Paré covered a lot of ground: he reintroduced the use of ligatures, based on his wide experience with gunshot wounds; devised trusses and artificial limbs; innovated in surgical technique; and he wrote pragmatically on obstetrics and the treatment of wounds. If medicine occasionally made real progress, it was through those rare labors, like Paré's, in the bewildering complexity of its science.

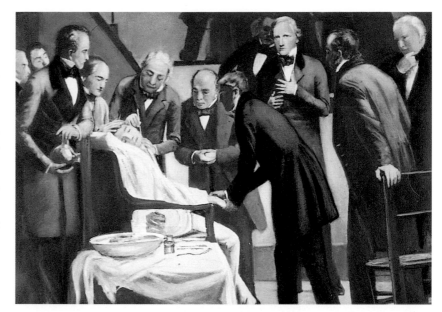

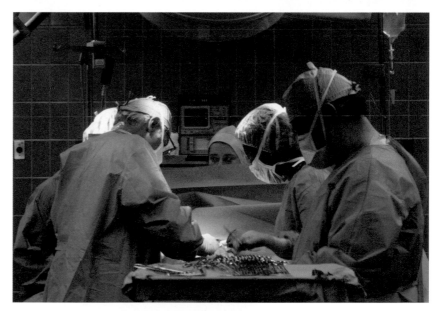

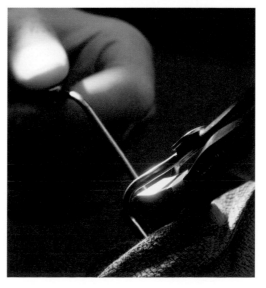

Top: A genuine milestone in medicine, the first operation performed with the patient under ether. The surgeon was removing a tumor of the jaw.

Above and left: The heirs to Harvey and Paré can now perform surgery with "knives" of coherent light—lasers—and on a scale visible only through operating-room microscopes.

René Descartes [1596-1650]

Descartes opened the door to the modern world—quite remarkable, since his works are barely known: a treatise on geometry, a handful of philosophical works, and a snappy phrase, *cogito ergo sum*, trotted out over and over in student coursework. Descartes was that rare genius whose medium was the message, and whose medium, or style, was so powerful that it captured the imagination of an entire civilization. And he did it in an age very dangerous to thinkers, deftly tiptoeing past Church doctrine when he could manage it, but seldom at hand when mere wit would not suffice.

René Descartes was born into a family of lawyers and doctors. At the age of eight he was sent to the Jesuit school at La Fleche. Because of a weak constitution he was allowed to remain in bed in the mornings, when all the other pupils had embarked on their day. For the rest of his life he continued to do the best part of his work in bed, and some might say this accounts for the meditative quality of his philosophy.

Thus the reclining genius grew to manhood, taking a degree in law in 1616. He pursued the life of a dilettante, signing up for one military expedition after another but rarely approaching a battlefield. He ended up in Ulm in 1619 where, presumably in bed again, he had a famous series of dreams. In the first he was lame, wandering in a raging storm and forced to take shelter in a church. In the second he heard the sound of thunder, a whirlwind of fire surrounding him. And in the last he opened at random a Latin poem, lighting instantly upon the phrase "what path should I take?" During his waking hours he'd been preoccupied with the method of analytical geometry; much unrealized potential there, he suspected.

Thinker and Dreamer

The dreams, the geometry, or perhaps the coincidence of both, affected him deeply. Not deeply enough to start work on the spot, but enough to vow a pilgrimage to the shrine of Our Lady of Loreto. He wandered about Italy, made the pilgrimage, and returned to France, where he attempted some mild scientific exercise. But he was soon distracted, sold off his lands, and reinvested the proceeds. During this period he befriended many of the Catholic scholastic authorities in France—throughout his life he would attempt to keep their friendly regard.

In 1628 he moved to Holland, where he was to spend the last twenty years of his life. That country was a haven for intellectuals, who enjoyed a certain anonymity and intellectual freedom—the Dutch had economic superpower status in the seventeenth century, and were completely preoccupied by commerce. He wrote to a friend, "the noise of their bustle does not disturb my reveries more than would the murmuring of a stream." In Holland he wrote and defended his major works. In 1637 he published a work whose ambitious title, *Discourse on the Method of Rightly Conducting Reason and Seeking Truth in the Sciences*, hinted at the greater scheme. The geometry appears at last, as an appendix to the *Discourse*.

Descartes began with the statement, "Any problem in geometry can easily be reduced to such terms that a knowledge of the lengths of certain straight lines is sufficient for its construction." This was an extreme shift from the ancient conception of mathematics. Since the days of the Greeks, geometry had been considered the highest intellectual activity. It was thought unchanging and aloof, the finest and most beautiful kind of abstract rea-

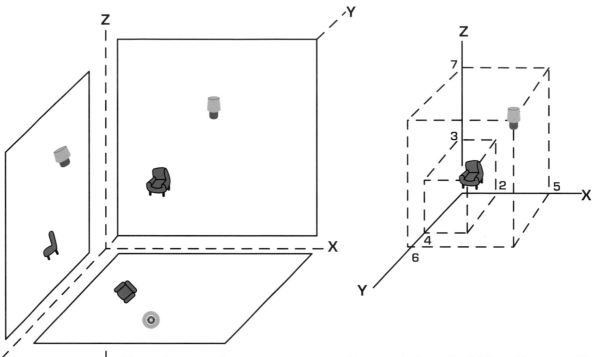

Cartesian coordinates: two views, with armchair at (2,4,3) and lamp at (5,6,7)

Above: *Though Descartes himself seldom used coordinates in the familiar rectilinear arrangement, the idea is clear: to unite algebra and geometry. Here, for example, two objects are "decomposed" by their coordinate numbers into various two-dimensional views. Within such frameworks, of any dimensionality, movement may be plotted, analyzed, and equations derived.*

soning. Through the centuries, mathematicians, notably Archimedes, had presented hybrid proofs that include arithmetical propositions. Archimedes himself apologized for their lack of rigor and beauty, but held that they remained interesting and useful.

Thus the tradition of so-called analytic geometry came down to Descartes, who awakened new interest by solving rather effortlessly in Book I an ancient geometrical riddle, the "problem of Pappas," concerning proportions among certain given lines. Descartes pointed out a little eagerly that neither Euclid nor Apollonius were able to find the nature of the solution.

The Greeks were positively addicted to constructing proofs with ruler and compass alone, and collectively exasperated over the unavailability of such proofs for the famous problems of trisecting an angle, squaring a circle, or duplicating a cube. Descartes's new method uncovered the futility of the Greek endeavors, for it was now obvious that geometrical problems whose algebraic equivalents are equations of the first degree have solutions requir-

ing straight edges only (essentially, adding lines together). Equations of the second degree need ruler and compass; anything higher, and not reducible, is out of reach of the preferred Greek instruments.

Lines, Equations, and Graphs

The magical power of generalization which makes all this possible, as Descartes pointed out, comes from uniting the algebra and the drawings. We can represent points and lines with magnitudes (numbers or letters), and represent them, furthermore, in parts, by assigning measures along graphic ordinates. And *this* is an equation. After explaining the basics, he said, characteristically, "…but I shall not stop to explain this in more detail, because I should deprive you of the pleasure of mastering it yourself." Or, we may infer, it was nap-time. Anyway, the gifted mathematician Pierre de Fermat had just arrived quite independently at the same place, so the world wouldn't have to take Descartes's word for it.

Truncated or not, the *Geometry* went a good way toward moving the focus of mathematics from the strictly aesthetic to

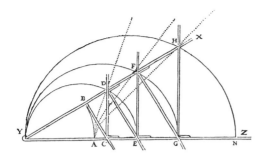

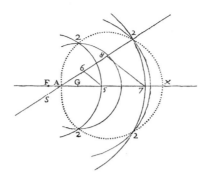

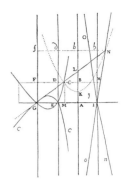

Above: *Diagrams (some solutions to quadratic and cubic equations) from* La Géométrie. *Descartes's treatise is the first whose mathematical symbols would be recognizable throughout to a modern student—except for his equal sign, which resembles a modern symbol for infinity.*

the useful. It introduced the coordinate system, in which points on a curve or line are expressed as distances from the axes, and hence become couples, triples, etc.—the familiar *x, y, z* characters of elementary algebra. Whereas the Greeks thought of geometry as direct apperception of the divine (which wasn't always around when they needed it), Descartes found readier approaches. In modern mathematics we are no longer doing so much contemplating of isolated properties of lines and figures; we are, effectively, behaviorists, who at a glance can not only read a curve's history, but also predict what it will do in proximity to other lines or figures.

Doubts and Certainty

Discourse on the Method is the seminal work of the modern age; and perhaps the only work of philosophy and theology whose subject is the author himself. It's an autobiography of the intellect, in which Descartes, either sitting in bed or by the fire, found himself thinking and doubting all that he could doubt. He remarked that all the preceding centuries of philosophy had not succeeded in establishing much as certain, other than the fact that we are a contentious species where our pride is concerned. There follows a general account of the way he tended to think about things, and, curiously, a list of his most important moral maxims: (1) Follow the laws and customs of my country. (2) Be firm and resolute in my actions. (3) Try to conquer myself rather than fortune. (4) Review the occupations of men to choose the best.

Now, in this meditative mood, he began to strip away all things open to doubt. He removed the evidence of the senses (for they cannot be trusted to give true impressions), and so dispensed with the external world. He conceived that he could have no body—and it disappeared. But he could not think that he didn't exist. As long as *something* is doing the thinking, he couldn't release the final bonds of existence and fly to the great bedchamber in the sky. Thus, "I think, therefore I am." He determined that this felt absolutely true to him, and generalized from it a distinguishing characteristic of true statements: "The things that we conceive clearly and distinctly are true." From this it was but a skip and a jump to: "man is the measure of all things," which was a particularly hazardous doctrine to profess in that epoch. But he quickly moved on to more universal matters. Through his doubting he felt at once the perfection of his thoughts, and yet something lacking at the same time. If he lacked, then Descartes could imagine, by contrast, a being who does not lack in any way—and here he adopted the ontological proof: If a truly perfect being could be imagined, then it *must* exist, since existence is rather more perfect than nonexistence. So, the thinking being, Descartes, got a roommate. After brief acquaintance with his new companion, and more philosophizing, he found his soul at last.

Not surprisingly, he was moved to ask himself whether inquiry is better conducted while awake or asleep. On the pro side of sleep, it can be done in bed; but

dreams may produce all sorts of illusions out of pure imagination, "and because our reasonings are never so evident nor so complete during sleep as during wakefulness…Reason tells us that since our thoughts cannot possibly be all true, because we are not altogether perfect, that which they have of truth must infallibly be met with in our waking experience."

In a subsequent work, *Le Monde*, or *Treatise of the World*, he introduced more controversial ideas, allowing that these matters were currently in dispute and it would be better "left to the decision of those best able to judge whether it would be of use for the public to be more particularly informed of them or not." Though this sounds like cringing, it was quite canny. Galileo had just been condemned and forced to recant for hawking the Copernican hypothesis—about Earth's rotation about the sun—and Descartes was about to employ the same thesis. *Le Monde* begins in front of his fireplace, with Descartes watching the ash whirl above the fire, which put him in mind of vortices swirling in the cosmos. He asked the reader to imagine a world, like ours in many ways, but unlike in others. Eddies of matter, vortices, in this other world

sweep the stars and planets around in their perfect motions. Descartes was splitting some hairs to get around the Church and Galileo at the same time. The Earth does not move, he claimed, but the vortex does, taking the obdurate planet with it. As he completed the furnishings of his alternate universe, disclaimers notwithstanding, it came to resemble our own in all its particulars. Through these strained subterfuges Descartes avoided prosecution for his unannounced, real purpose: destruction of the authority of the Schools and removal of the fetters restraining scientific inquiry. His philosophy, perhaps crude, is a basis for more rigorous attempts by David Hume and Immanuel Kant to create a sturdy epistemology.

In the last year of his life, Descartes accepted a commission to tutor the Swedish queen, Christina, in philosophy, which necessitated his remove from the agreeable refuge of Holland. Due to the queen's busy schedule, tutoring had to commence at the awful hour of five each morning, a time of day the poor philosopher had never in his life faced awake. After a few weeks of getting out of bed early in the cold Swedish winter, he caught pneumonia and died.

The Pursuit of Mathematics

I n the early seventeenth century it was beginning to seem that mathematics was the sort of thing gentleman did for recreation. Descartes fit it in between campaigns—on one of which, at the siege of La Rochelle, he crossed paths with another adventuring mathematician, Girard Desargues. Whatever the two of them may have discussed, nothing mathematical got settled. Descartes, of course, went on to lay out the method of analytic geometry; Desargues co-founded, with Pascal, the field of projective geometry, though his accomplishment was completely obscured for about two centuries. In fact, he did most of the obscuring himself.

Desargues had the fundamental theorem of projective geometry by 1639 (it concerns certain relations of triangles oriented in three-dimensional space). Instead of adopting Descartes's new coordinate system, he employed obsolete symbols, couched the work in freely adapted *botanical* terms, and wrapped it all up in treatise cautiously titled *Proposed Draft of an Attempt to Deal with the Events of the Meeting of a Cone with a Plane*. But for the discovery in the nineteenth century of a manuscript copy and the subsequent interest of J. V. Poncelet, an outstanding mathematician, there wouldn't be so much as a footnote left of Desargues. (There would be no Euclidean parallels "meeting at infinity" either; this convention originated in Poncelet's generalizing of the Desargues theorem.)

Another curious gentleman, John Napier, was dividing his time between religious tracts, weapons design (burning mirrors, artillery, armored carts), and inventing logarithms. The first two make sense in the context of the times: Napier, a Scot and a Protestant, had the deepest misgivings about the religious convictions of King James and the ultimate designs of Spain on the realm. Logarithms, however, amazed his contemporaries.

The concept seemed positively Einsteinian in its time, not the least because notations in use were a jumble; what might naturally suggest itself as a way to write exponents to, say, Franciscus Vieta need not crop up in the ciphering of Simon Stevinus. Also, what could it mean to raise a number like 10 (using it as a base) to the power .5 (equals 3.162), or .43136 (equals 2.7), or whatever? The solutions aren't intuitively obvious; in fact they involve a formula that generates a series, a string of terms that may be spun out to whatever length, and accuracy, is wanted.

Working with base 10 would have made some sense—Henry Briggs brought out this kind of "common" logarithm in 1624—but Napier's original version, appearing in 1617, was constructed on the truly confounding base 2.718281...(continuing infinitely), which isn't merely an *irrational* number (not exactly expressible in integers or fractions), it's *transcendental*: it can't even be obtained as the solution to any algebraic equation. This base, later acquiring the symbol e (for Leonhard Euler, Swiss mathematician), turns out to have many interesting properties, among them a surprising relation to another transcendental, π (*pi*).

Understandably, this went way over the heads of most people, thus the sense of bewilderment when Napier introduced a most practical application, his "Napierian bones," or "rods," the very first slide rules. Manipulating one of them the merest amateur, without even comprehending the mathematical principle, could perform almost instantly calculations that would tax an *idiot savant*. This compact device served science and engineering so well, it survived in use for 350 years, until supplanted by electronic calculators.

Above: *Two ways of representing the globe in a flat plane—projecting—points on a sphere onto a plane. Desargues labored on the theorems for this kind of operation, especially on the projective properties of conic sections—which, interestingly, happen to remain conic sections after projection. Obtusely (as usual), he characterized his conics as slices through a rolling pin, another bit of doomed terminology.*

Blaise Pascal [1623-62]

44

Pascal, a practical man when he chose to be, made a famous wager in his *Pensées*: Whether or not one believes in a heavenly paradise, the value of eternal happiness is incalculably high. Therefore, leading a religious life in the expectation—however small—of winning the stakes is always an odds-on bet. At best a sporadic theologian, Pascal scores higher as a mathematician.

A Child Prodigy
Pascal's father, a philosophical sort, believed that mathematics shouldn't come too early in life and deferred the subject to the age of sixteen in the plan for his son's education. The young Pascal, at twelve, seems to have proved certain Euclidean theorems on his own, which got the curriculum quickly revised. At sixteen he was working on his own theorems, contributing in that year his *Essay on Conic Sections* and another beautiful result—still known as Pascal's theorem—on an invariant projective property of an inscribed hexagon.

Later, Descartes would be openly skeptical of these achievements at so early an age. (The two disliked each other and actually met only once.) Indeed, he hadn't come so far altogether unaided; his general precocity in his studies had convinced his father to bring him along to the weekly gatherings of notable intellectuals under the sponsorship of Marin Mersenne in Paris.

Pascal rather easily absorbed the awkwardly presented geometrical ideas of Girard Desargues, a regular at Mersenne's "academy," and leapt ahead, essentially creating projective geometry as a formal discipline. A working knowledge of projection certainly existed well beforehand, in rules for map makers trying to flatten the globe or artists making perspective drawings. The subject may be thought of as studying all the shadows a figure might cast when illuminated from different angles by a beam of light and searching out qualities that remain recognizable—as perhaps the unchanging identities of lines or planes of intersection. In its generality it departs from the precise geometry of measured distances and angles, attributes not usually conserved in projections.

Two years later Pascal turned to a more practical end, the invention of a mechanical calculator. After building fifty modifications of his somewhat over complex design, by 1645 he had a machine that

Below: Pascal, a versatile genius envied by Descartes and studied by Leibniz, is often reckoned history's greatest mathematical might-have-been. His life was too brief, too full of afflictions both physical and spiritual.

would add and subtract, even if a bit stiffly. With the exception of a prototype device made by Wilhelm Schickard in 1623, Pascal's is the first automatic calculator known, and he put his into production, with respectable sales. Pascal didn't have to depend on his projects for an income; his widower father provided for his son and two daughters from his government salary and perquisites as a tax commissioner and judge.

Altogether it appears that Pascal's energy and genius should have been able to flourish in full degree, leading him where it might. But the paradise he recommended staking one's life on is not of this world, especially if one of your sisters is a spiritual bully. In fact, Pascal had not only a pious sibling (Jacqueline) but lifelong dyspeptic pain and insomnia. At his sister's urging he adopted the Jansenist creed, a cold collection of doctrine seemingly held together by an overwhelming hatred of Jesuits. In this spirit he was later to compose the famous *Provincial Letters*: sharp, skillful attacks aimed at the Society of Jesus. During his periodic obsessions with faith, mathematics would be laid aside, resulting in a net contribution that seems effortlessly brilliant but truncated and diffuse.

Weighing Air

It was in 1647, while enjoying a few years of abated torment, that he joined the scientific controversy over the vacuum. Did it really exist? Aristotle, of course, said no; nature abhors it. Torricelli said yes—he'd begun work on the problem with modern physics' first great experimentalist, Galileo, during the last year of Galileo's life. Torricelli had just died and Pascal took up the work, with no loss to scientific method. Unconvinced Aristotelians posited that an especially pure component of air seeped through the walls of glass apparatus so that a true vacuum was never allowed to form. Even the less dogmatic minds among them found absurd the clear implication

of Torricelli's results, that air has weight.

In a definitive series of experiments, Pascal directed that a mercury-filled barometer be carried to the top of a prominence in Auvergne, with readings noted during the ascent and compared against those indicated by a second barometer stationed at the starting point. As predicted, the height of a mercury column does fall with increasing altitude as the pressure of air supporting the column decreases, proving that air has weight and Aristotle has correspondingly less. Later experiments correlated barometer values with changing weather conditions. Besides settling the immediate questions, the investigation led Pascal into further work in fluid statics.

Above: Pascal's definitive experiments to establish the material, massy nature of air—at the same time proving the genuine emptiness of vacuums—led to further work (seen here) in hydrostatics and his invention of the syringe and hydraulic press.

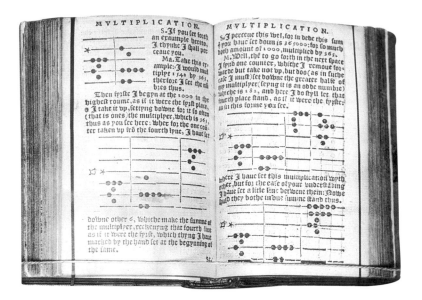

In 1651, on the death of their father, Jacqueline repaired to Port Royal, a Jansenist center, and entered a convent. Pascal was able to pursue his interests with more than his usual vigor until a carriage accident brought on a thoroughgoing conversion in late 1654 sending him packing to Port Royal as well. But before shutting himself away he had corresponded with the finest mathematician of the age, Fermat, and they jointly founded the study of probability. Pascal's interest had been aroused, apparently, by questions put to him by the Chevalier de Méré, a professional gambler with a keen interest in the answers.

Above: The fastest way known in Europe to perform arithmetic, before Pascal's machine, is demonstrated in this textbook, used by William Shakespeare. Diagrams illustrate techniques of shifting markers around on a counting board.

Right: The calculating machine devised by Pascal needed some design tinkering to make its long train of linked gears move with sustainable effort. The tinkering continued, evidently, after his death, for Leibniz was showing off an improved version (which he claimed was his own) to the Royal Society in 1672. Numbers are dialed in on the rotors and a result read from the windows at the top.

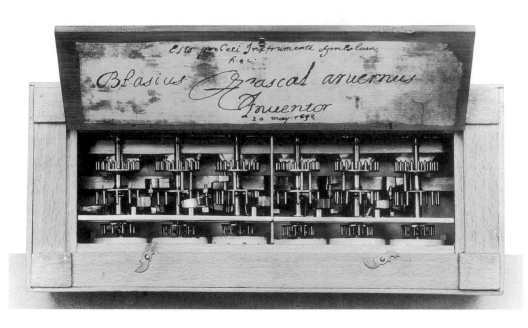

Specifically, Pascal was asked to find how the stakes should be divided between two dice players if a game should be suspended before reaching its conclusion.

Throwing the Dice

The answer, Pascal saw, must depend on a mathematically determined *expectation* of the winnings of each player—but in what sense might various outcomes be expected? He began by tallying the num-ber of ways in which each outcome could be obtained. With a single die this amounts simply to observing that six outcomes are possible, the numbers one through six, and that each can occur in only one way. With two dice combinations must be considered. Whereas a total of seven may appear in six ways, for example, three comes up in only three ways out of the full thirty-six per-mutations of two six-sided dice. In this kind of work Pascal occasionally employed

Left: Pascal's life and work are summed up neatly in this illustration: the objects of his pursuits, his thoughtful pose, and the dominating icon over his desk. The cone at his right elbow is marked as if to section out of it a hyperbola— much of Pascal's math-ematical work concerned the properties of conics.

Above: The Cheats, *by Georges de la Tour. Most gamblers probably don't have a sure grasp of the odds, but in Pascal's day the information wasn't available even in theory. Of course, getting a tip on an opponent's hand or a peek at the cards, as here, works better.*

the number triangle that bears his name; as well as giving the coefficients to a binomial expansion, the rows indicate how many unlike pairs of things may be chosen from a collection of four, or five, or six, etc., different objects.

Neither Pascal nor Fermat had much difficulty working out rules for combinatorial analysis, but they diverged in their approaches. While Fermat worked more directly at deriving probabilities, Pascal was more concerned to link the results to correct decision-making for gamblers, more pertinent to the practical questions of de Méré. Given a certain range of probable outcomes, how, Pascal asked, should a gambler divide and risk his stake to expect, with mathematical justification, the best results? In this respect, Pascal anticipated uses of probability not really explored until the twentieth century.

In the course of exchanging results with Fermat, Pascal almost casually defined a method of proof, mathematical induction, which has both become fundamental to mathematics and a source of contention in the philosophy of the subject. It's a two-

step process, easily illustrated with some simple addition. Intuitively we have no trouble asserting that any two numbers (a, b) added together may be added to a third (c) and a fourth (d) or any succession of numbers (n). Mathematically, this is the same as saying $a + b \ldots n$ works no matter how far the operation is extended. For a logical proof, as Pascal organized it, what's needed is *induction*, assuming a more general case by bringing n into it, and then showing that what works for n also works for $n + 1$ in a "hereditary" way. It's shorthand for a chain of reasoning with a lot of "therefores" in it, demonstrating that something, if true for a, is necessarily true for b, and if true for b, is necessarily true for c, and so on. The condition that's inherited is the validity of the implication from each to its successor. If successors can be related in this way, if something true for any value of n must be true also for $n + 1$, then the proof may be considered as applying to all n.

The problem with this, in the eyes of some modern schools of analysis, is that it terminates at infinity. Mathematicians have always been divided on the proper way to handle infinity. Cantor's direct grappling with classes of infinity in the late 1800s caused the nearest thing to an international mathematics scandal that's ever likely to happen. Some theorists would like to find equivalent proofs that don't bring infinity into the picture, or simply do without. As the distinguished logician Quine said, that's like "mathematizing with both hands behind one's back." As for Pascal, he rallied himself only once more from the severity of religious contemplation. In 1658 he published discoveries in the abstruse field of number theory and, under a pseudonym, rather bizarrely circulated questions in a mathematics contest to which he contributed his own answers. The pain returned, worse than before. Among the findings at his autopsy, in 1662, was the presence of a brain tumor.

Fermat's Beastly Scribble

Fermat, Pascal, and Descartes tend to dominate any narration of pre-calculus (*i.e.,* pre-Newtonian) mathematics, which is perhaps as it should be. But this shrinks and paralyzes history, like a specimen in formaldehyde. Nothing ever really goes forward by neat paragraphic leaps, certainly not mathematics and physics. A considerable body of work had already been done, in problems belonging to the calculus, probability, number theory, algebraic methods, etc., by exceptionally able minds.

The fundamental theorem of calculus was probably known to Torricelli by the 1640s (and Galileo was thinking about infinitesimals during his last years); Newton's teacher, Isaac Barrow, published a serviceable version in 1670. John Wallis had a method for the areas of parabolas in 1655. If asked to name the world's leading mathematicians, a knowledgeable Englishman of the period would have probably started off with James Gregory and Christiaan Huygens and perhaps worked down a list much less familiar today: Vieta, van Heurat, Cavalieri, Oughtred, Hudde, van Schooten. Fermat, easily the best of the generation, should be somewhere on the list, too. In terms of priority, his creation of a method to find tangents (1629) is significant, but his work only emerged slowly—he was a hard-working and respected magistrate for whom mathematics was a stimulating sideline.

As well as a durable and brilliant body of mathematics, Fermat left behind one special torture for future analysts, "Fermat's Last Theorem." It wasn't unusual for the busy magistrate to leave hasty notes in the margins of his books. Next to the eighth problem in Diophantus's second book of arithmetic, Fermat had scribbled the equation was insoluble and "I have discovered a truly wonderful demonstration which this margin is to narrow to contain." Specifically, the exercise is to find any whole numbers or fractions that solve the expression $x^3 + y^3 = a^3$ or any similar expression where the exponents have the value three or higher.

Now, many of Fermat's results in number theory were presented without formal proof—it was just his method—yet later mathematicians found them consistently provable. Undertaking to dispose of the cubic problem, for which Fermat here claims he actually knows a proof, leads into unexpectedly deep mathematical waters. The enigma has engaged nearly every amateur at one time or another and seriously stalled a few promising professional careers. Gauss, no mere mortal and peerless in the theory of numbers, eventually pronounced Fermat must have deceived himself, that whatever proof he had in mind must have been defective.

Of course, that didn't end the matter. Quite recently (1994) a proof of the Last Theorem has been given by Andrew Wiles of Princeton University, a proof that's been received well by the onlooking mathematical world. But Wiles's demonstration runs over two hundred pages, and alas there are one or two details....Anyway, this rambling wilderness cannot be what Fermat had in mind. The points for elegance are everything in mathematics. Will anyone be satisfied that Fermat's challenge has been well and truly met? Well, no one much cared for Gauss's view of the matter, either.

Left: The arithmetic triangle, often called Pascal's triangle, appears in mentions and sources dating as far back as the eleventh century. This version belongs to a thirteenth-century Chinese text, Precious Mirror, *by Chu Shih-Chieh. Pascal proved some novel theorems on its properties but, more significantly, made the first rigorous use of mathematical induction in one of his demonstrations.*

Isaac Newton [1642-1726]

Below: Newton's orrery: though clearly not to scale, this kind of mechanical solar system can be set up to reflect relative planetary positions during observation or calculation. The terms of Newton's Lucasian professorship actually required him to make his instruments and apparatus available to other curious scholars.

Opposite: Newton investigates the mystery of light with a hand-held prism and a quarter-inch hole drilled in the shutter of his study. The rainbow effect was well known, but Newton's thorough method and reasoning quite exploded the standard Cartesian explanation.

Nearly three centuries removed from the world as Isaac Newton knew it, we can't really feel the excitement and magnitude of his contributions. The laws of motion, of gravity, of forces, the calculus have endured long enough to seem quite ordinary, even dated, by the standards of modern physics. If, by mid-seventeenth century, many indicators pointed to an inverse-square law (and several versions are imaginable) it still took a genius to find the one expression that most simply united planets, moons, tides—and everything that falls.

As at other critical times in science, the need for new explanations had become apparent. Unlike the impasse of physics in 1905, when experiment had forced theory into seeming absurdities and required Einstein to put things back together; or again in 1913 when Bohr salvaged the incomprehensible dynamics of electrons; optimism abounded in this earlier age. The problems facing Newton were more basic, inasmuch as he must create a new branch of mathematics just to start work.

Clockwork Toys and Personal Study

The beginnings of this colossus were inauspicious. He was born prematurely; his mother remarked that all of him wouldn't fill a quart mug. From the age of three, upon his father's death, until age ten he was cared for by his grandmother, his mother having contracted a marriage with an elderly, well-to-do bachelor. Of his schoolwork we hear nothing, no legends of precocity, although it's known he constructed ingenious playthings, miniature mills, clocks, sundials. The curriculum at Grantham Grammar School appears to have stirred nothing of his genius, at least not until he'd plowed through a good many books on his own and coincidentally realized that he would need some recommendations to proceed further. He left Grantham in 1661 for Cambridge University as first in his class.

Happily, he was to attend the lectures of Isaac Barrow, the first holder of the Lucasian Chair in mathematics, who had worked principally on methods of calculating areas and finding tangents to curves. These are the fundamental problems of

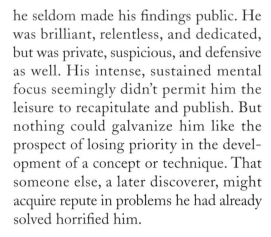

what we now call the integral and differential calculus. Newton could hardly have planned a more fruitful preparation for the project ahead of him. In another fortunate twist, courses were suspended for two years during one of those periodic outbreaks of plague to which Europe had resigned itself since the first calamitous epidemic of the fourteenth century. Newton spent the interim at the family estate, Woolsthorpe, in Lincolnshire.

As his school days suggest and later achievements bear out, Newton was at his very best when left alone. His notes—which were copious—indicate that in this solitude he propounded the calculus and the universal law of gravitation, not to mention the binomial theorem and a theory of optics which accounted for the splitting of colors in a prism. Curiously,

he seldom made his findings public. He was brilliant, relentless, and dedicated, but was private, suspicious, and defensive as well. His intense, sustained mental focus seemingly didn't permit him the leisure to recapitulate and publish. But nothing could galvanize him like the prospect of losing priority in the development of a concept or technique. That someone else, a later discoverer, might acquire repute in problems he had already solved horrified him.

Privacy vs. Pride

Time and again, Newton hurriedly made public that which his natural closeness had confined only to his notebooks. When Mercator, in 1668, published a treatment of infinite series, Newton immediately communicated his own methods, far more wide-ranging and useful, which he had arrived at several years before. He disputed with Huygens the origin of a theorem on circular motion; his own delay, as usual, was to blame. In a most celebrated clash, he contended with Leibniz over creation of the calculus. Evidence shows that both independently worked out a comprehensive system—Leibniz's had an advantage in the clarity of its notation. Newton, on this occasion at least, satisfied himself with an exchange of letters. Somehow the matter grew, caught a patriotic fire, and intruded itself even into decidedly unmathematical company—the public doesn't very often rally round the calculus. Years later Newton appointed himself to write the verdict for an English committee set to referee the claims. The decision, in favor of Newton, came as no surprise.

The Calculus

Newton and Leibniz put modern mathematics on its feet, but left a good many loose ends to be tied up. Calculus, in brief, depends on making some generalizations about *functions*, most often encountered as equations relating the values of one or

Left: Newton at eighty-three, a formidable intellectual figure even in the last year of life.

more *variables* to another variable. That is, equations usually prescribe a way of manipulating a value of one variable, say *x*, to come up with a new value, say *y*. Any set of mathematical operations may be specified in getting from *x* to *y*: whether it be by addition, subtraction, or multiplication. It is the *form* of those equations that calculus analyzes—*e.g.*, is anything squared, cubed, or divided by another variable? The actual numbers that might be solutions are of secondary interest to the method. (In fact, finding numerical answers to some of these reworked equations can be next to impossible; solving such problems, or even obtaining good approximations, is a mathematical specialty in itself.)

As it turns out, there are often shortcut ways of inspecting and altering an equation which allow for adding up all the values the function has taken on as *x* gets larger or smaller—like an instant cumulative readout. Newton called it the method of "fluxions." If the function happens to be traced out as a curve on a graph, just such a sum of its values from each point to the next gives the area enclosed by the curve—a very handy operation, known as *integration*. The converse, called *differentiation*, involves rules for rewriting the equation so as to give a "speed" of the function: how fast it is growing at any

Below: In the culminating, crucial experiment to prove that prismatic color components in white light are quite separate—not mere modification of a basic, pure white state—he directed the spectrum (from prism ABC*) through a lens (* MN*) and recorded at various distances the spectral color spread, its white recombination, and its continuation to an inverted arrangement of the colors.*

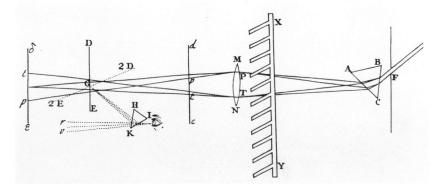

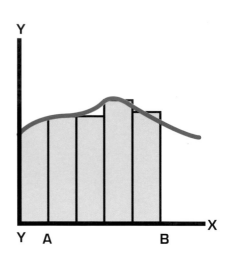

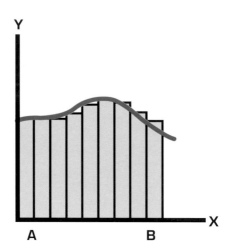

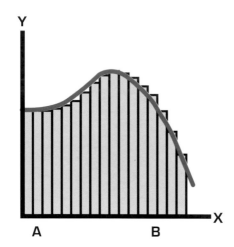

Above: Conceptually, the integral calculus finds the area under a curve by covering it with ever closer approximations, or more accurately, the limit toward which such an impossibly long sum tends.

Right: In differential calculus the problem is to find the tangent at any point along a curve, a "slope"—as if the curve were made of infinitely small straight segments. This is useful to determine, for example, where a curve has reached a maximum or minimum value, for only there will its tangent be perfectly flat, with a slope of zero.

point. Again, using curves, differentiation provides a measure of relative steepness anywhere along its length. There are, unfortunately, few hard and fast rules for discovering these shortcuts but, with a few theorems and a mathematician's intuition about where to look, an immense body of formulae has been worked out since Newton introduced his fluxions.

Amazingly, these formal manipulations occasionally uncover deeply buried relationships. From a mathematician's point of view, this is a great improvement on mere problem-solving by arithmetic or algebra. Functions go in one end and concealed similarities, identities, and unifying principles come out the other—sometimes anyway, although most solutions aren't very dramatic.

Powerful as these methods are, and inestimably useful, the fundamental proofs rely upon slippery numbers called "infinitesimals." No matter how successful the results, professional mathematicians worried over defining "infinitesimals" for two centuries, tossing them out in favor of "limits," and have since shown signs of wanting to bring them back again. One can't help thinking that to Newton such discussions would have seemed to turn merely on points of faith.

The Mechanics

Cambridge's self-effacing Barrow resigned his chair in favor of Newton in 1669. Newton ventured to publish a tract on light and color in 1672, but found scholarly discussion and defense of his work burdensome. He might have been left to his increasingly alchemical and theological contemplations if the astronomer Edmond Halley hadn't asked to see a proof of elliptical orbits Newton claimed to have worked out many years before. Perhaps he felt another of those torments coming on, a priority of place being pulled away. At

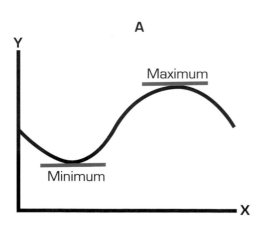

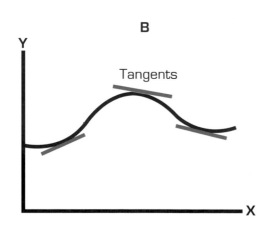

Left: It is a considerable leap to imagine that gravity, so uniformly oppressive at Earth's surface, practically vanishes at large distances. Newton's initial thoughts on the problem were bedeviled by a simple error of approximation (for the nautical mile) in his rough calculations.

Below: Tiny (nanometer-scale) variations in soap bubble thickness fraction light into whorls of color.

any rate, in working up the nine-page demonstration (*De motu*), something drew him into that characteristic Newtonian absorption and he didn't look up again for a year, until he'd finished *the* masterpiece of modern science.

The manuscript of *Philosophiae naturalis principia mathematica* (usually called the *Principia*), arranged in three books, was delivered in April 1686 to the Royal Society for publication. The Society, unfortunately, had thrown its ready cash into a lavish *History of Fishes* that hadn't sold well and couldn't assist. Halley paid for the first

Above: *The tale of an apple falling to Earth and crystallizing the form of universal gravitation in Newton's mind is one he put about only in his last years. It's certainly an attractive scenario but was perhaps streamlined in the telling; at least, his notebooks show a theory incomplete for nearly a decade after that solitary period of his life.*

Above, right: *Billiards is Newton's physics in a nutshell—inertia, force, momentum—and a fequent metaphor for a perfectly mechanical universe. More recent developments (concerning computability, chaos, and quantum uncertainty) make clear that even billiards cannot be so completely determinate as in Newtonian thought.*

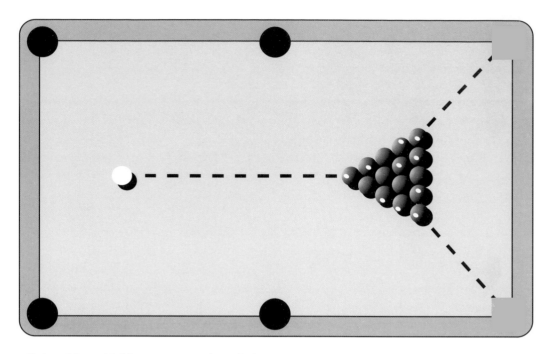

edition himself. Newton introduced the work with the famous three laws of motion: first, a body continues in a state of rest or uniform (unaccelerated) motion unless acted upon by an external force; second, acceleration of a body is proportional to the force acting upon it and in line with that force; and third, for every action there is an equal and opposite reaction.

The first law really states a definition of *inertia:* that property of matter which resists forces. No one knows *why* things have inertia, although theorists continue to work at an explanation. The second law yields the most basic of equations in mechanics: $f = ma$ (force equals mass times acceleration). The third warrants that momentum carried into an interaction is the same as that carried away. Momentum is conserved. Quantities may get redistributed, but nothing is gained or lost overall. Working upon this basis, Books I and II analyze a compendious range of forces and motions, including a remarkable treatment of wave behavior.

Newton writes, at the beginning of Book III, "I now demonstrate the frame of the System of the World." The heart of the work is the law of universal gravitation, a thing of beautiful simplicity:

$$f = G \frac{mm'}{d^2}$$

Which is to say, the attractive force (f) between two masses (m, m') is directly proportional to their product and inversely proportional to the square of the distance (d) between them. The constant of proportionality, the gravitational constant (G), is one of the pillars of science, alongside such verities as the speed of light and Planck's constant. With this straightforward and compact expression, we may calculate, for example, that an average chocolate fancier and a 100-gram bonbon, one meter apart, attract one another with a force of about a half-billionth newton—a newton being a unit for measuring force. (If nothing disturbs this purely gravitational experience, they'll collide in sixteen years.) And the equation applies equally well to vegetables, tides, planets, and distant galaxies.

The constant G, by the way, is usually given as 6.6732×10^{-11} Nm/kg, in units that make no intuitive sense but cancel out with the masses and distance in the equation. Small letter g mustn't be confused with the universal G: it's convenient, when you live on a fairly large planet, to solve the equation with one of the masses—the planet itself—already figured in. This gives the ready-made value of acceleration at its surface. So, at Earth's surface, a distance of one radius from the planet's center, the attractive force works out to 9.8 meters per second-per second, which is g. (Newton actually had some difficulty proving that distance, d, should be computed from the center of mass of a large object, *e.g.*, from the center of the Earth.) At greater distances from a planet's center, perhaps in orbit, g dwindles until accelerations from other gravitating masses, most notably the sun, predominate.

The *G* Controversy Goes On

The universal G, unlike g, never varies anywhere in the cosmos, as far as we know. Its value is directly correlated with the total of all mass in the universe. Measuring it, over and over, has become a preoccupation of modern physicists, as well as devising theories that might lead in a natural way to obtaining its value. Some conjectures require a universe in which G grows smaller with time, weakening by a trillionth or so each year. Experiments seem at present to confirm its constancy to a slightly greater accuracy than the needed change. Newton found G—someone else will have to explain it.

Assured at last of a resounding priority in nearly everything that touched on physics, Newton found himself no longer able to work beyond the public eye. He had become visible. Stature took him to Parliament and into public office, first as Warden and then Master of the Mint. Indeed, England gained probably the best Master of the Mint that ever filled the office; thus moth-balling one of the greatest minds in history. Or, as the mathematician E.T. Bell once wrote, "The crowning imbecility of the Anglo-Saxon breed is its dumb belief in public office or an administrative position as the supreme honor for a man of intellect." The fire of his concentration never left him. When Bernoulli and later, Leibniz

offered at large some troublesome mathematical problems, Newton had the solutions within hours. While studying the anonymously-submitted proof to his own exercise, Bernoulli exclaimed, in the traditional translation, that he "recognized the lion by his claws."

Above and below:

Newton's scientific imagination enlarged the human cosmos, bringing us for the first time within range of those universal harmonies sought by Kepler.

A Secret World of Pseudo-Science

Below: Newton's unnerving concentration suffuses a portrait by artist and poet William Blake. Newton approached alchemy with the same intensity as the puzzles of physics.

The personal library Newton left behind numbered 1,752 books; of these, 369 were scientific works and fully 170 treated magical subjects: divination, alchemy, myth, occult philosophy, and those secrets each age has supposed belonged to the "ancients." Newton spent weeks at a time, usually alone, performing obscure experiments in his Cambridge lab. Humphrey Newton (no relation), an occasional assistant, mentioned taking turns to keep the furnace stoked night and day. Could this Isaac Newton be the author of that mechanistic perfection usually called the "Newtonian world?" Or should he be seen, as John Maynard Keynes once asserted, as the last of the great Renaissance magicians?

Commentators on Newton, particularly in the past, often treat this aspect of the great man as an aberration, on a level with the mental breakdown he experienced in the early 1690s. But the chimerical researches that so consistently occupied Newton throughout most of his life, including during his most productive periods, cannot be dismissed. To begin with, Newton's natural intensity begot in him an intense faith. His scrutiny of scripture, with special attraction to the prophetic texts, led to his scathing rejection of tra-

ditional doctrine and organized clergy. A bit of a conspiracist, eccentric, occasionally obsessed, he wouldn't be denied a glimpse behind the veil. His quest for the secret knowledge of things spiritual went forward with the same tireless energy and seriousness as his inquiry into physical phenomena.

Neither is it clear in the seventeenth century where mystical alchemy ends and empirical science begins. Whatever Newton hoped to discover, he set about it with exemplary method, reading everything available, compiling a five-thousand-item index under nine hundred headings, and testing his authorities in the fire. To him, the subject was a fortress of age-old secrets, a place where unknown causes might be at work. Alchemy, almost by definition, had been a hermetic, hidden pursuit. Alchemists through the ages had confided only in one another and, generally, only on the informal basis of trading a secret for a secret (or trading magic for gold—selling insider tips made as good a wage in the Middle Ages as it does in the present day). The texts are apt to be couched in arcane symbols and indistinct metaphor, with a generous proportion of nonsense and abject fantasy. A principal challenge for Newton was certainly decoding the materials.

Newton had already penetrated into the physical universe as far as anyone of his century. He never believed that sort of knowledge would enlighten him on the nature of life and of the mind or even, indeed, as to the substance of things. He was publicly defensive about his private experiments; his rare observations on alchemical results were offered with no intent to discuss or uphold. In this regard, he is often compared to his friend Robert Boyle, a fellow investigator in practical and impractical chemistry. Boyle, however, embraced an open search for knowledge, from whatever source derived; embarrassment wasn't in his nature. In Newton's phi-

losophy, with its mystic regard for the ancients, rumors of such things as a hidden "higher geometry" were handled with sober attention. And, how much more improbable could the ciphered tracts of Flamel, Trismegistus, Sendivogius, or della Porta seem than René Descartes's statement that "there is nothing visible or perceptible in this world that I have not explained." By the measure of more conventional philosophy, alchemy must have seemed, on the whole, a modest and manageable inquiry.

Above: A symbolic incarnation of the element mercury. Newton's obsession with alchemy's arcana reflects a natural secretiveness and eccentricity as well as a fascination with the process of experiment. He constructed most of his own equipment, steeped himself in the literature, and plotted his own course.

Karl Friedrich Gauss [1777-1855]

It is sometimes lamented that Gauss hadn't spared more time for number theory, or electromagnetism, or topology. Everything could have been found out fifty years ahead of time and who knows what a head start like that might have done for the world? Poor Gauss! He worked ceaselessly from the age of seventeen until his death, leaving so much of the overflow of his results in his diary and correspondence that mathematicians for two succeeding generations acquired the nervous reflex of searching his notes before daring to believe they'd discovered anything new.

Gauss was the archetypal genius, complete with all the dramatic touches generally bestowed only in fiction. Born in poverty to the family of a bricklayer, he performed long sums in his head at age three, taught himself to read, and committed tracts to memory. His photographic memory would hold for effortless reference such things as log tables and the many languages Gauss absorbed. (Languages and literature were his hobbies, so that he invariably read the major works in their original texts—including Sanskrit.)

At the age of ten, as the story goes, he solved an exercise given to his class—a dreary iteration of sums—by intuiting the notion of a series, evident in the problem, and obtaining its result within seconds. After this performance, he was allowed to find his own way under the tutelage of a gifted enthusiast, J.M. Bartels, not much older than Gauss himself. The providential notice of the Duke of Brunswick allowed him to continue his studies, at the Caroline College and the University of Göttingen. The good Duke Ferdinand provided him a yearly stipend after graduation, when it became clear that a teaching situation would only hold Gauss back. Gauss never desired much more than a quiet study and a good chair. Time was all he coveted.

Number Theory

Gauss was reckoned by his mid-twenties among Europe's foremost intellects. Though he published little, the work he submitted always drew the fullest attention of the mathematical world: in Gauss his contemporaries recognized a wellspring of creativity. When he presented a subject, it would fly in new directions, at least for those who could digest the rigor and beautifully honed terseness of his proofs. His first large treatise, *Disquisitiones Arithmeticae*, unified and generalized disparate elements of pure number theory. He composed the subject into a sublime landscape of congruences—not for casual viewing, though: the treatise, in seven sections, has been sometimes referred to as the "book of seven seals." In later years the mere fact of Gauss's interest in a scientific topic carried the presumption of significant results.

Major world events intruded briefly into the work of this genius. Gauss's patron, Duke Ferdinand, commanded the Prussians at Austerlitz, Auerstedt, and Jena—a string, as history records, of brilliant French victories. The Duke was badly wounded at Jena and died in the next year (1806), leaving Gauss without a sponsor and without an income. As Gauss had recently and quite blissfully married, the loss was doubly serious—and threatening to the prestige of German scholarship, since Gauss received immediate offers from as far away as St. Petersburg.

The influential Alexander von Humboldt, adventurer and scientist, suggested Gauss for the professorship of astronomy at Göttingen, though not without first

Left: The great Gauss, a genius with a quirky personality. Critics argue as to the value of the voluminous notes he hoarded and maintain that his tastes in reading—in several dozen languages—ran to the ordinary. Nevertheless, his achievements were indisputably extraordinary: as well as leading the field of pure mathematics, he discovered the asteroid Ceres and applied himself to research and invention in magnetism, optics, surveying, and acoustics.

doing some homework. In another of those tales that attach to genius, it is related that von Humboldt inquired of the French eminence Pierre Laplace who was then the greatest mathematician in Germany. Laplace nominated J. F. Pfaff, at Helmstedt, a good friend of Gauss. Put off his stride because Laplace hadn't endorsed the name he proposed for the candidacy, von Humboldt asked about Gauss. "Ah," Laplace clarified the obvious, "Gauss is the greatest mathematician in the *world.*"

Indeed, Gauss occupied the position at Göttingen for the rest of his life. The exac-

tions of an occupying army ceased with Napoleon's blunders of 1812. His wife had died in 1809. He remarried and settled into work at Göttingen, troubled only occasionally by the obligation to instruct a few students. He concentrated at first on the world's leading astronomical problem: determining the orbit of Ceres, the first of the asteroids to be discovered in 1800. The difficulty, inferring the complete motion from a limited number of observations, was both a theoretical and computational morass. The method he developed was definitive.

Magnets, Maps, and the Telegraph

Over the years, he delved as deeply into practical physics as into mathematical structures: surveying, measurement, optics, map-making, and electromagnetism. He directed a survey of the region, including a fine analysis of local variation in the terrestrial magnetic field using instruments of his own invention. In the course of this project, he developed a familiar procedure for evaluating observational error, the Gaussian distribution, or "bell curve." He invented an electric telegraph in 1833—some years before Morse's patent—using it regularly to communicate with fellow scientist Wilhelm Weber. From time to time additional polished masterpieces appeared: seminal works on hypergeometric series, complex variables, elliptic functions, differential geometry, conformal mapping. Gauss was never out of his depth. Shelved with the enormous unpublished residue were the makings of whole new fields, among them well-formed anticipations of non-Euclidean geometry and topology.

Discovering Non-Euclidean Geometry

The story of non-Euclidean geometry is somewhat tangled, there being three claimants to the honor of its discovery. The other two, Nicholas Lobachevsky and Johann Bolyai, seem to have reached similar conclusions around 1823. Lobachevsky published first, in 1829, and Bolyai in 1833, but Gauss had been mulling the idea decades earlier. Undoubtedly all had worked independently toward the same result, but the coincidence was probably thrown with loaded dice. Lobachevsky, an outstanding mathematician and teacher, studied at the University of Kazan under Bartels, Gauss's great friend and early tutor. Bolyai was the son of another lifelong friend, Wolfgang Bolyai, who instructed Johann in mathematics. That a shared curiosity about Euclid's validity should thus be transmitted doesn't seem

so curious; that all three concurred in their reasoning, however, was remarkable, underscoring the soundness of a very counterintuitive result.

Of Euclid's ten axioms, one (the fifth, concerning parallel lines) had never sat well with mathematicians; it was the cause of a vague discontent. Nine of the axioms seemed simple and obvious, like "the whole is greater than any part," or "all right angles are equal." As stated by Euclid, axiom number five practically requires a diagram. Classroom texts usually make do with an equivalent proposition holding that through any point, one, and only one line may be drawn that is parallel to another line. (Even this simplification suggests the need for a diagram.) By this definition, Euclid gives parallel lines the unique property of never meeting or crossing.

Any number of mathematicians, including Gauss, had satisfied themselves that the other nine axioms couldn't be combined to prove the postulate about parallel lines. So, like all axioms, it must be accepted on faith as a fundamental truth. But is axiom number five necessary? Non-Euclidean geometry begins by assuming a replacement axiom for parallels, listing it with the other nine, then investigating the geometry that results. As it turns out, no contradictions crop up, so the new system is valid.

Gauss *et al.* adopted an axiom of multiple parallels, *i.e.*, that more than one line drawn through the same point may be parallel to the given line. While the geometry can be developed without looking at figures, it's useful to picture how this can happen. Indeed, we have to dispense with flatness in the usual plane of Euclidean proofs.

On a surface that is everywhere growing and curving away from itself—a saddle-shaped surface will do—lines in the plane are carried away from each other as well. Some of them will never intersect by virtue merely of being spread away from each other by the plane's curvature. In fact, for every classical Euclidean parallel ("one and only one parallel line") there is an infinite family of lines that won't intersect a given line. They all go through the same external point, as per Euclid, but don't splay enough ever to approach the given line. Thus, we have a case against Euclid, though only by warping, literally, Euclid's common-sense flat planes.

These multiple parallels are really curved lines, it would seem, not the straight ones Euclid dealt with. But inasmuch as "straight" lines necessarily take on curvature whenever a "flat" plane is unevenly stretched in some way, we are completely justified in continuing to think of them as straight. Not every line, after all, would straighten out as the surface is "relaxed" to its previous flatness, only the kind that can satisfy the alternative parallel axiom. Specifically, if as Euclid held, a straight line is the shortest distance between two points, these apparent curves have that property on this surface. In a mathematical sense these lines remain as uniquely identifiable (*i.e.*, "straight") as are the familiar straight lines of Euclid and everyday drawing exercises.

Although the remaining nine axioms still hold in the new system, some of the theorems utilizing old axiom number five must be tossed out. For example, the angles within a triangle no longer add up to 180°; the total is less. In fact, the sum depends on the *size* of a triangle: the farther "straight" lines are extended across this kind of surface, the more severe their curvature at some future intersection, and thus a smaller angle at any junction with another line. Triangles with three equal angles are no longer merely similar, they are fully congruent—the bare sizes of the angles in this geometry imply the traverse of a certain amount of curvature and hence the sizes of triangles.

Flatness and Curvature

The new theorems immediately raised questions in Gauss's mind. How can we assume so readily the real world is fundamentally Euclidean? There's no *logical* reason to choose flatness over curvature. The triangles of experience are pretty small compared to other possible frames of reference like, say, the rest of the galaxy. If

Below: Triangles projected from three-dimensional surfaces with negative and positive curvature. On the 3-D surface, each triangle "edge" is the shortest distance between the points it connects; projected to two dimensions, the "straight" lines become curves, and the angles of each triangle add up to either less (negative curvature) or more (positive curvature) than 180°. Ultimately it doesn't matter much whether we think of geometry as possessing an ideal "flatness" or a curvature, as in these examples.

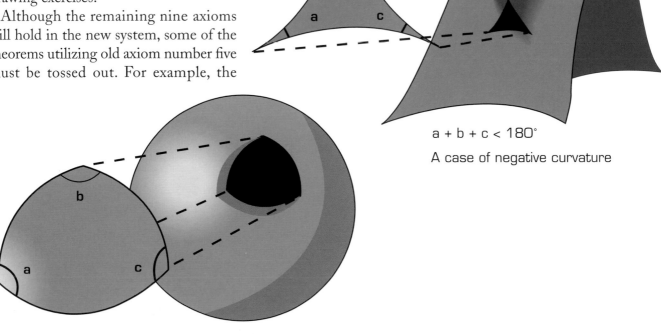

a + b + c < 180°

A case of negative curvature

a + b + c > 180°

And the positive condition

space itself were somehow curved at a large scale, we'd probably never stumble across the evidence: small triangles on a suitably enormous Gaussian surface would diverge from 180° in their angular sums by an undetectable amount. Nonetheless, Gauss determined to triangulate some widely separated points (mountain tops) to see if any appreciable disparity arose between the Euclidean expectation and the data.

The real question, of course, is how did Gauss get so far ahead of his age? Even the purpose of the experiment could only be communicated to a few mathematical friends; he himself was amused by the bizarre aims of the test. Within the limits of observational error, he established nothing—which meant to Gauss that the question remained unresolved for larger or more accurate measurements. Were he given a large enough laboratory to work in, say some region of the universe, the results might have surprised even Gauss. Later mathematicians have shown that the angular sums of triangles would turn out greater, not less, than 180°. This is the relativistic form of non-Euclidean geometry.

The geometry of Gauss, Lobachevsky, and Bolyai uses a parallel axiom that implies, mathematically, negative curvature. Taking another position on parallels, that *none* may be drawn through a given point, leads to positive curvature. A use-ful surface for visualizing this idea is that of a sphere: its straight, "shortest-distance" lines are great circles—which always intersect. The sphere's geometry deranges Euclidean theory—eliminating airy extensions of lines to infinity. All straight lines become loops (all have the same length, as well); perpendiculars intersect; and as is true in the negative case, angles in triangles depend on area, though increasing as area grows.

The positive case is a creation of the great mathematician Bernhard Riemann, after whom the structure is usually termed "Riemannian geometry"—a just tribute. The young Riemann had to deliver his all-important doctoral lecture before a panel that included Gauss himself. Furthermore, Gauss had personally selected the topic from a list of three Riemann submitted—although the foundations of geometry appeared last on the list. Not only did Riemann have to work feverishly to perfect his notes, he suspected that Gauss had some deep interest in the subject, and this loomed over his preparations. (Fear of the omniscience of Gauss seems almost an occupational neurosis among his mathematical contemporaries.) Happily, the lecture was brilliant, Gauss was impressed, and Riemann did put together a geometry that, since Einstein, is believed to underlie the reality of space.

Right: The telegraph that Gauss invented served well enough to communicate with Weber, several rooms away, but was never improved for wider, practical use.

Getting Sublime

The nineteenth century was a golden age for mathematics—fittingly, ushered in by Gauss. Though brilliant minds, from Galileo and Newton to Euler and Lagrange, had enormously enriched the study, in truth the perimeters of this field were being enlarged by sporadic acquisitions. The fantastic extent of its territory was revealed only by their successors, a veritable mob of first-order analytical talents. All of mathematic's traditional branches, like geometry, number theory, algebra, etc., were spruced up with new rigor, wider perspective, and gaps filled in.

Families and hierarchies of the abstract emerged: when by the end of this incredible century David Hilbert announced his famous, and doomed, program to put some finishing touches on the invisible edifice, the problems he proposed were chiefly of a metamathematical nature—proving theorems about theorems. This is the level at which the remotest kinds of mathematics had arrived. Riemann's reflections on geometry, to give a typical example, led him eventually to generalizations of all geometries, subsumed in the rules that related them through certain invariant properties.

Whole new fields, like group theory and mathematical logic, were soon producing interlinked group spaces and families of logics. Another new discipline, topology, so denatured the substance of measure and form as to become a mathematical ameba in the plane of the ideal—all that counts in topology are notions of "betweenness," or "right of," and "left of." But it turns out to be the most powerful way, mathematically speaking, of expressing the difference between a doughnut and a baba au rhum.

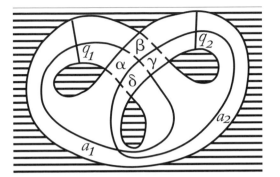

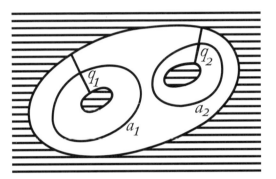

Left: Some topological pretzels from Riemann's work: the object is to distinguish among surfaces by the kinds of "connectedness" within the interiors. Things that matter are types of possible paths (a's) and how many cuts (q's) are needed to reduce a pretzel or an anchor ring to an elementary unholed surface.

Often in mathematics, though, the most ordinary things resist all solution. Mathematicians from Archimedes to the present have been tormented by the obduracy of prime numbers. Most would trade some part of their isomorphically transforming souls for a peek at the truth. To wit: how many primes are there in a given interval? Or, given a prime what rules can locate the next or any subsequent prime? Even a method for confirming a prime without having to try all its possible factors would constitute a triumph. The ground is littered with broken conjectures and tantalizing observations. Equally deep is the mystery of why it should matter. Isn't this an obsessional hangover from the childhood of mathematics? The discipline has grown so much since the time when an irrational number could put a Pythagorean off his food; how deep could one more theorem run? The answer, of course, is that no one knows.

Michael Faraday [1791-1867]

That Michael Faraday should have come to play a major part in our fundamental understanding of nature is surely the most ramshackle piece of good luck in the whole history of playing at long odds. Born into poverty, malnourished in childhood, rudimentarily educated, broadened only by incidental reading in the chance lot of books delivered for rebinding at his place of apprenticeship, taking as his guide a motley of obscure writings in science and moral self-improvement—everything in Faraday's life seems to hinge on plot elements borrowed from Dickens. He countered at every turn almost comically bad turns of fate with his earnest determination to do better.

An Amateur Chemist

Faraday's blacksmith father had to desert his own failing smithy for the vicissitudes

Right: Faraday at the height of his powers was the most gifted experimentalist of his century. He gave to physics the accomplished fact of a field theory, though without its mathematics. In this illustration he is posing with a battery.

of employment in London. Of the early years little is known. His parents followed a nonconformist religion, the Sandemanian doctrine, which placed its reliance in the more positive interpretations of scripture: simplicity, charity, community. Faraday remained in the faith his entire life; indeed, Queen Victoria provided him a house at the close of his life, as it was well known that Sandemanians didn't allow themselves to hoard or save up wealth.

From his years apprenticed to a bookbinder he took away the commendable precepts of *The Improvement of the Mind*, the work of one Isaac Watts, a clergyman with an irrepressibly positive and practical view of how to get on in the world. Inspired by Watts, Faraday began attending lectures, copying out his notes, helping organize a discussion group—never flagging in trying to learn more. His passion was chemistry, and the public lectures

of Humphry Davy at the Royal Institution his curriculum. When Davy temporarily blinded himself in 1812—through a touchy chemical reaction—Faraday was recommended for the short-term secretarial position that opened up. Soon thereafter, in another quick adjustment of fortune in his favor, he filled a lab assistant vacancy at the Royal Institution.

Under Davy's tutelage, Faraday took in the leading theoretical concepts of the day, often encumbered as they were by topheavy philosophical schemes. As it turns out, Faraday possessed a great fire for ideas, but was hesitant about propounding theories of his own. Partly, perhaps, he followed the reliable Watts, who advised making the most accurate and extensive observations before hazarding an opinion. It's also true Faraday had no mathematics beyond arithmetic. His finely quantified experiments in chemical and electromagnetic analysis were

Above: Faraday's lab at the Royal Institute as it appeared around 1870. Though mostly given over to chemicals, the workplace also contains various pieces of his electrical apparatus, at the right, on benches and the floor.

Above: In the grand amateur spirit of the age, audiences thronged the lectures at the Royal Institute. The Prince Consort, Albert, and sons are present in this rendering. Faraday was the star, presenting his discoveries with natural clarity and practicality.

prompted by some quite nonmathematical sense of the underlying principles and entities. He was never comfortable explaining his own intellectual approach; his writings set out the most striking ideas, though with all the ambiguity and convolution of extended metaphor. His papers were seldom fully noticed or digested when they appeared. Such larger conjectures as he permitted himself, with almost timorous reserve, he sealed up in an envelope in 1832 that remained unopened until seventy years after his death.

The immediate results of Faraday's employment at the Royal Institution were the loss of one journeyman bookbinder to the trade and the making of a first-rate chemical analyst. He accompanied Davy and his wife on an eighteen-month tour of the Continent (1813–14), taking in the scientific sights and personages along the way. Within a few years—and married now—he was drawing occasional fees for

outside work and expert court testimony. In the course of discharging such commissions, he discovered benzene (1825), borosilicate glasses, and several high-grade alloys of steel—Henry Bessemer took Faraday's work as a starting point in developing his commercially practical process. (A court appearance, unhappily, occasioned a great rift between himself and Davy; they testified for opposing sides in a sugar refining dispute.) Though significant, these investigations were eclipsed by the researches, begun in 1821, in electricity, electrochemistry, and electromagnetism.

Initial Discoveries in Electromagnetism
"On Some New Electro-Magnetical Motions, and on the Theory of Magnetism," published in October 1821 in the *Quarterly Journal of Science*, describes the first conversion of electrical into mechanical energy. Faraday had made a bar magnet rotate around a fixed current-carrying

wire, and the reverse, fixing the magnet but not the wire. The stunning implication, a complete theoretical novelty, is that magnetic poles can move, continuously, in an immobile piece of the apparatus. To interpret the result he posited circular "lines" of magnetic force radiating from the current carrier. In this is the germ of all physical "field" theories: treatment of certain forces as distributed through *space*, and with mathematically describable intensities. Faraday could not, of course, give mathematical form to these most percipient inferences, but they separated him from the electrical mainstream, partial at this time to exclusively fluidic models. The muddle is evident in Hans C. Oersted's fuzzy description of the magnetic force surrounding a current—he discovered the phenomenon—as an "electrical conflict."

Throughout the ensuing decade Faraday tried to improve the concept suggested to him by experiment, arriving at a picture in which the effects propagated as "strains" in and around material particles. Whatever the form, he thought it probable such forces must interact; a strain in one wire should disturb the state of another, if sufficiently close. With this in mind, and with his unique working knowledge of electricity, he performed experiments in 1831 which inaugurated electromechanical technology on one hand, and the theoretical line of inquiry that leads to relativistic physics, on the other.

His first demonstration uses two separate, insulated wires wound around opposing halves of the same iron ring (iron concentrates magnetic force, as he already knew). Passing a battery's current through one wire, he expected, would build a magnetic influence that would set current flowing in the nearby wire. But the idea isn't wholly accurate, and the experiment would have been a dud except that Faraday noticed his galvanometer, connected to the second wire, twitching

whenever current through the live wire was turned on or off. A few weeks later he had the full solution: current is induced to flow in a secondary circuit by a *changing* magnetic force. Two quickly arranged experiments confirmed his thinking. In the first he slid a magnet in and out of a wire coil, thus constantly varying the strength of the force actually cutting across any part of the coil; the galvanometer registered a variable but continuous current. For the second he constructed the world's first dynamo, a copper disk mechanically spun edge-on in the gap between poles of a magnet. A current began to flow in a circuit through the copper disk.

Altogether, Faraday had conceived and proved electromagnetic induction, and incidentally disclosed the form of devices that converted mechanical to electrical energy, or the other way around: dynamos and motors. Further, his initial induction ring configures a third basic electrical component, the transformer. It didn't set the world on fire at the time and he himself had difficulty clarifying his notion of force lines, though he never abandoned the view. Real support didn't arrive until 1845, when William Thompson (the future Lord Kelvin) wrote to say he'd found a mathematical treatment of the incorporeal lines and to suggest further research. In the meantime Faraday had turned to other troublesome issues in electricity.

The Role of Electrical Charge

Many disparate happenings could make a galvanometer's needle swing: a spark between plates of a Leyden jar (static electricity), the constant discharge of a voltaic pile (battery), temperature differences between thermocouple junctions, and even some species of eel. No real effort had been made to unify them as an expression of the same fundamental force. By ingenious means Faraday united static and constant discharges through their equivalent action in the decomposing of water (electroly-

Above: Faraday proved that manifestations at immensely different scales, lightning discharges and battery currents, evince the same electrical properties. He made, in effect, the as yet unposited electron a logical necessity.

sis)—which led to another brilliant series of discovery and inference.

Faraday built a strong case for a wave-like, "vibratory" transfer of positive and negative elements through substances in electrolysis; a continual combining and recombining of components with a net drift of the *effect*, not the molecules themselves, in the direction of the respective electrodes. He called the tendency an "exaltation of the affinities" electrically present in the material, which gives some idea of how hard Faraday's thinking can be to keep up with. This ran counter to the prevailing picture of substances being sundered by electrical forces and pulled piecemeal to the attractive poles. Faraday's molecules are hardly moving, though some forceful quality is clearly felt and passed along. As Hermann Helmholtz pointed out forty-five years later, Faraday's results by 1834 admit no logical explanation save that of a point charge, *i.e.*, an electron.

The experiments were summed up by Faraday in his famous laws of electro-chemistry: the total quantity of current applied determines how much of the substances in solution will be separated (or deposited on the electrodes, which is the same thing); and the amounts of substances deposited will be in the same ratio to one another as in their chemical composition—expressed in relative weights, *e.g.*, water is oxygen and hydrogen in the weight ratio 8:1. Faraday, and later Helmholtz among others, saw how strongly these facts argue for electrical charge as the fundamental force for the binding of atoms together into molecules. It is, as we now know, the entire basis of chemistry.

By 1838 Faraday had all the elements of a complete electromagnetic theory: the movement of charge without dislocation of matter itself; *curved* lines of force— how unlike classical examples, such as gravitation; quantitative convertibility of

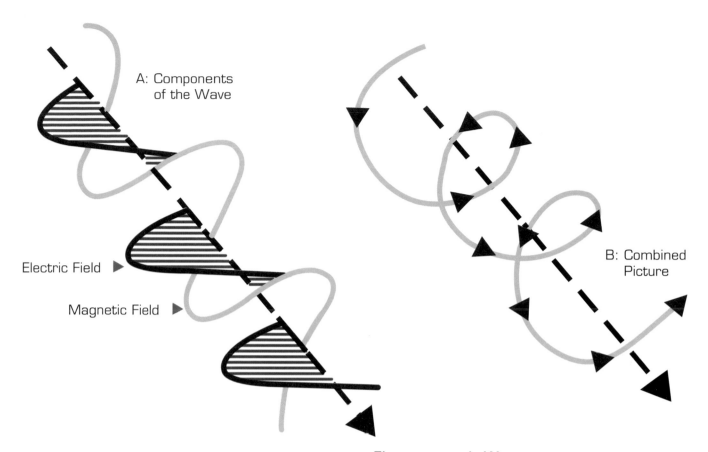

A: Components
of the Wave

Electric Field ▶

Magnetic Field ▶

B: Combined
Picture

Electromagnetic Wave

chemical, electrical, and mechanical energy; the unity of all electrical phenomena. By 1839 his mind was a shambles. He suffered an illness or breakdown of some kind and was never again able to concentrate with the same intensity. Much of the old acuity returned briefly in the mid-1840s, but a gradual decline had set in. The debility was apparent to him, and he removed himself by degrees from former associations. Conserving what he could of his vigor for lecturing at the Royal Institution, particularly to young audiences, he resigned at last in 1862. Within a year or two he was scarcely able to stand or speak.

Tricks with Glass

In those last active years, 1844–46, he bridged a final, formidable gap in that lifelong program he'd set himself: to unify natural phenomena. Using glass of high refractive index (fittingly enough, the kind

he'd created in the 1820s) he succeeded in rotating polarized light within a strong magnetic field. That is, light filtered so as to contain only those waves lying pretty much in the same flat plane was pulled up at angles, as Faraday reports, proportional to the amount of magnetic force applied. This, and subsequent discoveries about how well different substances concentrate or resist magnetic field lines (paramagnetism and diamagnetism), is the electromagnetic world as Faraday left it.

He could hardly have been aware through the 1850s and 1860s of the magnificent job James Clerk Maxwell was doing to give mathematical expression to his discoveries. No doubt the equations would have looked alien to him, but not the fields which they describe. In this we have some assurance from Faraday: the envelope finally unsealed in 1937 revealed his firm conviction that electromagnetic waves would be found.

Above: *The undulatory nature of electromagnetic emanations—usually called waves—is conceptually most like a corkscrew. Total energy doesn't really rise and fall but is maintained in cyclically varying proportion in electric and magnetic phases.*

Field Work

Faraday's experiments and papers, insofar as they penetrated the scientific establishment, brought some strange news to physics. Newtonian particles and masses had existed in splendid isolation, acting on other presences from a distance and occasionally bouncing off one another when paths intersected. Expression of the forces between them as straight lines had a certain mathematical bulk, but was not taken as particularly *real*. Not that "action at a distance" didn't embarrass physics: ever since Descartes' proposal of dynamical "vortices" to materialize the forces of nature theoretical swarms of etheric principles inhabited the void. Faraday's forces, however, are stored and transmitted in palpable fields—abstractions perhaps, but abstractions that can move solid things around.

The brilliant James Clerk Maxwell, who was to give Faraday's electromagnetism a breathtakingly coherent mathematical form, entered physics with a flurry of work on such topics as color vision, optics—he invented the "fisheye" lens—and a description of Saturn's rings (calculating a gravitationally permitted locus and the necessarily fragmentary nature of the rings). He was fortunate in the circumstances of life, coming into possession (by an especially tortuous inheritance through an illegitimate line descended from the eighth Lord Maxwell) of the family's 1,500-acre estate in southwestern Scotland. Educated at Cambridge, he returned there in 1871 as the first professor of experimental physics; he designed the famous Cavendish Laboratory.

His name will forever be associated with a rare thermodynamical creature of his imagination, Maxwell's demon, a "very small, *but* lively being incapable of doing work but able to open and shut valves which move without friction or inertia." Sounds like a perfect bureaucrat, but one that could serve physics in building up an otherwise impermissible amount of order in gas molecules, sorting them out by energy. Such a beast is completely mythical.

Maxwell's field equations are a very different matter; the point is in just how real they are. Working them out took several years—after all, the four basic equations embody diverse experimental findings accumulated over nearly a century. The idea of fields belongs to the mathematicians, unconcerned about their practicality. Seamlessly folding natural phenomena into physically demonstrable fields—previously unheard of—belongs to Maxwell.

The mathematics, partial differential equations, spreads the influence of electrical charges in a particular way through surrounding space. For any point, the immediate direction and intensity of force—actually two kinds of force, magnetic and electric—is calculable. And every point may be examined through time as well, giving a plot of change in the field as conditions evolve. The equations unify, moreover, magnetic and electric strengths as related expressions of a single kind of energy, electromagnetism. What comes out of the equations depends, of course, on what's put in. Given initial values, like amount and direction of current, or several currents, a complete picture of the resultant electromagnetic field emerges. With extensions of the method provided by H. A. Lorentz the mathematics can be run backwards too, predicting (reasonably well) the behavior of charged particles, *i.e.*, a current, in a given field.

The most remarkable demonstration of the equations' power is a solution that calls into being a radiative wave of energy. Magnetic and electric forces in such a wave propel each other along by alternately building up energy in an electrical field, then swapping it into a magnetic field, and so on, back and forth with each successive wave crest collapsing to feed the next. The magnetic and electric wave components exist spatially at right angles to one another and are 90° out of phase. Just as one attains a maximum strength, the other reaches a minimum.

Mechanically, the wave may be thought of as a pair of flywheels driving each other up to speed by turns, except these flywheels lose no energy to friction. This smooth, oscillating exchange of form can go on forever, unless the wave interacts with something and is absorbed. Maxwell was even able to calculate how fast such disturbances should travel in his fields—and it turns out to be the speed of light.

Here is discovered the nature of light. Mathematical performances like this don't come along every day. And the equations by no means limit energy propagation to the arbitrary, tiny range of wavelengths between 380 and 800 nanometers, which is visible light. Heinrich Hertz detected the first of the invisible frequencies, radio waves, in 1888. The rest of the spectrum, from radio to gamma rays, was quickly completed.

Below: Inspection of superconducting electromagnets for the behemoth underground Supercollider, a particle accelerator project now indefinitely postponed.

Charles Darwin [1809-1882]

Below: *The* Beagle *off the South American coast. Its master, Robert FitzRoy, was a keen thinker who greatly stimulated Darwin over the five-year course of that famous voyage.*

Opposite: *Charles Darwin, though chiefly remembered for the theory of natural selection, spent far more time compiling enormously detailed monographs on such subjects as barnacles, molds, coral reefs, and various families of plants.*

In the mid-nineteenth century, it must have seemed to any science enthusiast, everything was finally getting settled. Fragments of an elusive whole lay everywhere, innumerable advances were cropping up in every corner of rational inquiry. If electricity and mathematics or a bit of thermodynamics wouldn't explain it all, then someone would have to look through a microscope or a telescope, or build a new machine altogether, but it was all getting done. Given this march of insight, invention, and discovery, the news of human origins should have been complacently anticipated. The headline probably should have read: "Humans finally learn the truth about humans," but instead ran: *The Origin of Species by Means of Natural Selection, Or the Preservation of Favored Races in the Struggle for Life.* The author, of course, was Charles Darwin, who managed to get the entire thesis into the title—usually shortened to *Origin of Species.*

Gentleman and Scholar

Darwin was born into the right end of England's highly stratified society, the son and grandson of distinguished physicians. His mother was a daughter of the ceramics magnate Josiah Wedgwood. Though intended for medicine by family tradition, Darwin veered into general studies at Christ's College, Cambridge, with a view to preparing himself for the Anglican clergy. He was diverted once again, in 1831, by an invitation to sail with HMS *Beagle*, a survey vessel bound for the south-

Below: Darwin as a young man. He wrestled perhaps too long with the details of evolutionary theory, hoping for a comfortable fit with conventional moral views, but quickly followed up the tardy appearance of Origin of Species *with* The Descent of Man, Variation of Plants and Animals Under Domestication, *and* The Expression of the Emotions in Man and Animals.

ern coasts of South America. The *Beagle* had a scientific mission: to gather up specimens—plant, animal, fossil—and make geologic notes. Not only was Darwin well up on the natural sciences, for which he'd found a great affinity in his university courses; but as a gentleman naturalist he could be expected to pay his own way.

The voyage lasted five years, exploring South America, the Galápagos Islands, Tahiti, and coastal Australia. Darwin returned with crammed notebooks, thousands of details of the peculiarities of species: behavior, form, habitat, population. He may have brought back, as well.

a blood parasite vectored by a member of the assassin beetle family, the benchuga bug. He believed so, at any rate, and attributed to it his generally weakened health in future years. His mental pace never slackened, however. Darwin seemed to engulf everything in view, storing away prodigious amounts of material, organizing and reorganizing it in encyclopedic trains of thought. But by 1838, he hadn't yet tied together his *Beagle* observations into a scheme; his reputation was simply that of brilliant geologist.

Transmutation or Replication?
The big biological question at this time, for Darwin and other naturalists, was how far resemblances among species could be taken. Varieties, sometimes extreme in expression, occur within species; dachshunds don't at all resemble Saint Bernards, but they can mate successfully. Between different species, though, reproduction fails. If this is the case, how could one species beget another? Much of what was known in fossil and living animals suggested "transmutation" of species, a transforming of some part of one into another, yet the mechanism couldn't be demonstrated. Some observers favored a fixed species list, without transmutation, where others searched for an arrangement that was more fluid.

Transmutation implies some kind of evolutionary view. Indeed, the idea had been kicked around since Jean-Baptiste Lamarck first gave it theoretical form in 1801. The difficulty comes in trying to imagine how it might work. Lamarck endowed his species with a special "vital force" pushing development in beneficial directions. Some noted thinkers had taken up a "gradualist" or "evolutionist" position, including Herbert Spencer, Ernst Haeckel, Alfred Russel Wallace, and Richard Owen. Darwin's own grandfather, Erasmus Darwin had written on the need for supposing that individual "creation" events did not tally with the evidence. Owen, for example, could not fathom the extreme localization of some species as part of a Creator's intervention; does it make sense to be always conjuring up, say, a new species of grouse just to inhabit this or that island alone? Would the Creator be so much of a geographical window dresser? Also, if a Creator did indeed start off with a species portfolio, why had it become so hard to find boundaries past or present between mere variations and true species? By degrees gradation, modification, divergence, and such were getting into the discussion.

The objectors asked of the gradualists why intermediate, transitional stages of development from one species to the next were uniformly absent (where is there a semi-bat or an almost-elephant?). How did such a highly specialized organ as the eye result from piecemeal development? The opposition had to stay on its toes, as the geologic and natural record provided new persuasion with every study of an obscure marine invertebrate or humble tree mold. The great Georges Cuvier, founder of paleontology and leading critic of evolutionism, retreated to an episodic form of creationism, in which the shelves are restocked with whole species after recurrent cataclysms in the Earth's history. His unifying idea, relating world-wide disasters to discontinuities in the fossil record, is a good deal better than ingenious; it's central to some modern investigations in geology and evolution of species. But cataclysms operate differently than Cuvier imagined, for the fossil strata show that species don't pop out of nowhere, and certainly not as part of a general plan of improvement, as he believed.

The Struggle for Survival

Darwin's insights appear to have started to crystallize after reading the 1837 *Essay on Population* by Thomas Malthus, the man who gave economics its reputation as the "dismal science." The Malthusian

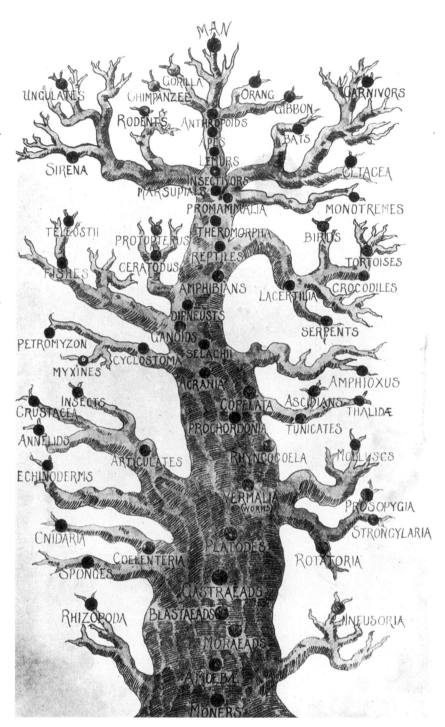

thesis, that population and food supply grow at disastrously different rates, impressed on Darwin the idea of struggle of competition for scarce resources. By taking nature to be, fundamentally, a contest between winners and losers, Darwin found a direction for the whole thing. Without some rules for rating the needs or success of species, an unceasing evolution of their forms, howsoever fascinating, made no

Above: A "Genealogical Tree of Man," the new perspective that necessarily flowed from Darwin's work. Many of Darwin's contemporaries found the implied nearness of man to mere chimps a confounded and irritating idea.

Above, right, and below:
Observing adaptation of species in the Galapagos Islands provided Darwin the clearest evidence for natural selection. The isolated environment is practically a natural laboratory for evolution of the native species, such as the iguana (one of five species on the islands) and blue-footed booby shown here.

sense. Now it was clear to him that species existed precisely because specific adaptations conferred a survival advantage—or *could* enhance survival prospects, if a particular new trait fit the survival bill for the animals or plants doing the evolving.

The advent of any new feature in a species that helps, say, a re-equipped fieldmouse stay ahead of predators (it could be better camouflage, greater speed, faster reproduction, or any number of things) will very probably ensure that neo-mouse descendants come to predominate in the fieldmouse population. If the older mouse type can't keep up, there will be fewer and fewer of them left to reproduce; they may die out. This explanation, as Darwin appreciated, gets along without a mysterious "vital force" or any intrinsic directives at all. Lamarck had the beginning and the end right, but he hadn't taken all the false starts into account. Darwin understood that myriad trait variations are *randomly* occurring all the time. When enough tiny modifications add up to a more efficient mouse—and *only* if they add up this way—"natural selection" takes place: differential survival rates work to buoy the efficient population and submerge the others.

This theory rather beautifully disposes of the question of intermediate forms. A successful variant will squeeze its own unmodified strain out of existence. The half-way forms and the whole ancestral line are doomed, unless of course they hold out in some habitat cut off, by shifting land masses or other reasons, from the newcomers. But then, those older population segments, too, continue to evolve; a completely different variant may arise among them, with a similar effect on the parent species. It would not be surprising that two (or more) quite separately evolved variants, though obviously related, could not interbreed because they have crossed the threshold into specieshood. This principle of divergence holds for any adaptive

1 *2*

3 *4*

Left: *In the Galapagos finches differentiated themselves from a seed-eating common ancestor into thirteen species, marked by adaptations of the beak to enable special feeding habits—narrower beaks for insects, broader for plant eaters.*

or natural event that divides species members: modification of diet, extremes of variation, incursion of other species, the dying of seas—nature devises endless scenarios. The very fluidity of the condition of life favors, even mandates, a continuous process of speciation.

The creationists, therefore, had been thinking backwards, which is easy enough to do even while talking in purely Darwinian terms. Species boundaries, the limits of reproductive range, don't exist to separate and preserve perfected examples of creation; they arise necessarily out of the very dismantling of previous species. Neither do species evolve, as the life-force crowd would have it, through a yearning to fill special niches—creatures working at improving their beaks, or fins, or knuckle joints. Species simply evolve by chance mutations, most of which have no discernible immediate effect, some of which are disastrous, and occasional long sequences of which put their possessors in good stead to outlast the competition.

Below: *Darwin taken in all at a glance: a series of skulls with a few of the intermediate steps from fish to man, evolutionarily speaking.*

It's one thing to say that birds evolved feathers in order to fly, and another thing to mean it literally, as Lamarck did. Grand evolutionary objectives are never in the plans of a mutating gene. Whatever the chain of modifications that led to feathers, many of them will have had some now irrelevant adaptive advantage, others will have been rather neutral at the time they appeared. The point is that change happens without any purpose; its value quickly gets rated by its ability to sustain life in its environment.

Below: The microscope in Darwin's study at Down House, the pleasant residence in Kent where he lived and worked for over forty years, until his death in 1882.

Publication of the "Big Book"

For reasons that no one has satisfactorily explained, Darwin took about twenty years to get his conclusions into print. He compiled revised drafts of the "big book" during the 1840s and then deserted them for

eight years to study barnacles. Only at a colleague's urging did he take the work in hand again in 1856. *Origin of Species* didn't appear until 1859. The precipitating event for publishing was a communication from A. R. Wallace, who had just prepared a paper reaching all the same conclusions. Not that Darwin was racing headlong for priority—recognition for his efforts mattered to him, obviously, but it took Wallace's disclosure to overcome whatever reticence or dissatisfaction had delayed him. He insisted, in fact, that extracts of his and Wallace's papers, the "announcement" of evolutionary theory, be read at the same meeting of the Linnean Society, July 1, 1858.

Origin of Species isn't quite the "big book" Darwin wanted. Its avalanche of examples drawn from every corner of the natural world may not yet have satisfied him. He continued to supplement the evidence in diverse later studies and in two especially ambitious tracts, *The Descent of Man* and *The Expression of Emotions in Man and Animals*. Without doubt, he created a stir from the top to the bottom of the literate public. The theory, while not wholly new, was controversial. Not that established religion had much trouble digesting it; evolution could just as well carry out a Creator's plan as any other natural means. But the loss of man's pristine descent rankled many, religious or not. The theory's scope and implications were even more massive than Darwin's notes.

Darwin had perceptively anticipated most scientific objections and offered some promising conjectures where they seemed necessary. But that wasn't the problem. He and a good many other thinkers enthused over evolution as a universal script, extending it into history, personal character, social and economic interaction. Herbert Spencer had been writing about a kind of social evolution since 1852. The notion fitted nicely into Victorian estimates of the way the world should be (which is to say,

British). Consequently, Darwin's fuller works are highly colored by a moralizing tendency—he had once aspired, after all, to join the clergy. "Survival of the fittest," Spencer's phrase, certainly also meant for Darwin survival of the most moral, the most high-minded, the "civilized" over the "savage." At the time, he wouldn't have liked his theory very much if it didn't affirm a Creator working at elevating the human race. (Later, he liked the theory of a Creator less.)

The smooth merging of natural selection into God's way of getting colonies staked out or wealth accumulated, sorting out the fittest with hearty congratulations all around—the tenor of what's often called social Darwinism—doesn't seem to a later age to be scientifically justified. Nor did it in his own day. Insofar as the storm over evolution touched on religion, contentions seldom got around to brachiopods; only in the twentieth century has controversy commonly involved scriptural attacks on the theory's scientific essentials. Those essentials remain intact. Darwin's great body of work and insight still anchors our understanding of natural history.

A Century of Evolution

Evolutionary theory has taken a beating over the years. No other part of science seems to have its power to bring heresy back into fashion. The *auto-da-fé* persisted only in glorious memory until John Scopes was consigned to the secular authorities (of Tennessee) in 1925 for teaching evolution in his classroom. Much of the public has decided, however, that one's descent—whether from apes, aliens, or mutating incarnations—must simply be put up with. The real question is, where does it all lead? And again, evolution gets an uncomfortable workout. It doesn't help that Darwin's own cousin, Francis Galton, conceived the notion of eugenics: selective breeding of the human race for improvement. Practical interpretations of this doctrine run from the merely chilling to transfixing horror.

Darwin's generation might be accused—like physicists in World War II—of putting a dangerous science into the wrong hands. It should have been obvious that evolutionary theory has the potential to blow up. On the other hand, does it actually require an advanced theoretical approach to make history as wretched as it usually turns out? Probably not. In any case, the comparison with atomic physics is too loose. What tends to unite biological evolutionary theory with grandiose social thinking is the simple breadth of the word "evolution," which serves well enough to describe change going forward in pretty much any context.

In its stricter, scientific sense, Darwinian evolution has been killed off in the press from time to time by announcements of its obsolescence, unsuitability, or fatal incompleteness. But reconciling the development of species to an ever larger fund of observation isn't smooth going. What's actually happening in the discipline modifies the generally steady picture Darwin preferred. Species do seem, in some examples, to undergo faster and slower periods of evolution; they also do things that appear only faintly adaptive. Rather than becoming obsolete, the theory is becoming richer. What the newspapers seldom have columns enough to print is that Darwin's evolutionary thesis remains in good shape so long as traits are produced at random and selection plays a dominant role in passing them along.

Paleontology, taxonomy, microbiology all converge strongly on an essentially Darwinian view, and so does mathematics. Only comparatively recently has it been possible to establish the "probabil-

Below: A case of evolution retracing its steps: this porpoise-like Jurassic specimen is Stenopterygius, *a saurian returned to the sea. Its limbs have become shortened and flattened, for efficient propulsion in the water. The dark outline of its body shape is quite authentic, actually a layer of carbon laid down with the creature as it fossilized.*

Left: *A member of one currently extant species surveys the colossal frame of a species retired from the active list a few hundred million years ago.*

ity" of species—including ourselves—evolving by a Darwinian route. Genetics has confirmed the all-too-mutable nature of the gene, but computers have charted the lineages.

Certain proteins—those most basic to life processes—occur in close but variant forms across many species; genes determine the exact make-up of any such protein for a particular species. As these variant proteins are long chemical sequences of amino acids, they may be sorted into a special order, putting at either end those needing the most amino-acid substitutions to turn one into the other. These are the cases most "distant" from one another. In between, still ranked by the rule of simplest substitutions, the others are inserted into place. The list will branch, too, at points where a single ancestral protein can best account for two dif-

ferent but close mutations. (Yes, evaluating all the ways the substitutions can be tried takes brute computer power.)

The final protein list reads from top to bottom as it should for the minimum of random gene mutations acting on the form of the protein produced; it's the least "busy" picture of a protein's transformation history. Now for the good part: such charts nearly always put species in the same order of descent as do other methods of studying them. But the computer knows, as well, a few million other ways of listing and branching the proteins. It can rapidly tabulate how much chancier, busier, other mutation paths must be to change the implied evolutionary order of species. And those are the odds; the numbers just shoot out of sight with any major hypothetical rearrangement. Scientifically, at least, Darwin is money in the bank.

Évariste Galois [1811-1832]

The history of mathematics has its sad tales—the early death of Norwegian mathematician Niels Abel or India's Srinivasa Ramanujan, the madness of Georg Cantor—but perhaps nowhere in the annals of genius was there a more tangled absurdity than the life of Évariste Galois. From the time he took up mathematics, at age thirteen, until his death seven years later, Galois's gift was variously misperceived as dullness, rebellion, conceit, and even plagiarism. He was twice refused admittance to advanced study by examiners unfit to judge him. On three occasions, leading mathematicians, in whom Galois finally reposed his hopes, miscarried, in one way or another, in bringing to light his best work. Just as he began to achieve his mathematical maturity, with less than a hundred pages published and profound ideas still crowding his mind, he was killed in a duel. In the space of a single night before the duel, he had hastily sketched his chief results. Truly, his fortune was a corrupted star.

Things started out well enough. His father, an amiable intellectual, directed a boarding school in the Parisian suburb of Bourg-la-Reine. Very much anti-royalist, he was elected mayor of the village during Napoleon's brief return from Elba and kept the post after the revesting of the monarchy. His mother's sentiments, too, were republican, though tempered by an austere, eclectic moral outlook. Well-read, outspoken, steeped in classical culture, she saw to Évariste's education until he was sent away to a preparatory school in Paris at age twelve. There he did well at first, despite an atmosphere he found oppressive and academically dreary. Eventually disgusted with endless drilling in the classics, and demoted, he digested on his own Adrien Legendre's *Geometry* and the major works of Comte Joseph Lagrange—challenging mathematics by any standard. (At age sixteen, he had presented himself for the entrance examination at the prestigious École Polytechnique but was found to have had insufficient preparation.)

A Genius at Seventeen

His extraordinary talent was finally recognized by L.- P.- E. Richard, an instructor in advanced mathematics. Of course, by this time, Galois was already preparing his first paper for publication. Stimulated by Richard's presentations and his own personal investigations, Galois at seventeen finally had a productive year. By May, 1829, he had written his finest theorems for consideration by the Academie des Sciences. France's leading mathematician, Augustin Cauchy, was assigned to evaluate the work and report to the Academie. He found certain parallels with Abel's results, advised some changes, but submitted no report to the Academie and, by some accounts, misplaced Galois' paper, as well. Galois did rewrite, including ground-breaking material in the theory of algebraic equations and submitted his work in February 1830, with hopes of winning the Academie's *grand prix* in mathematics. This time the evaluation was given to Jean Baptiste Fourier, but Fourier died shortly thereafter. Galois's paper was never found, and he was peremptorily dismissed from the competition.

Meanwhile, Galois had enrolled in the college for preparing secondary teachers, the École Normale. His father committed suicide in July 1829, apparently despondent over a campaign of slander against him waged by local clerics. In the next month, Galois again was denied admission to the École Polytechnique, but this time the examiners were clearly a good

Left: A portrait of Galois engraved sixteen years after his death, from a juvenile portrait drawn by his brother Alfred—a very second-hand kind of immortality and about the best history can do for this tragic genius.

deal denser than the candidate. In frustration, he is reported to have thrown an eraser at one particularly obstinate questioner. Things went no better at the École Normale. He was expelled in December 1830, for writing an article strongly criticizing its director. Galois had been drawn into the popular agitation against the Restoration government, including its eager minions in school administration.

In January 1831, he had a last try at the *grand prix*, this time with Simeon Poisson as referee. (Poisson is best remembered for deriving some mathematical rules of probability based on the incidence of death from mule kicks.) The paper contained the most complete demonstration yet of his new theory of groups applied to settling

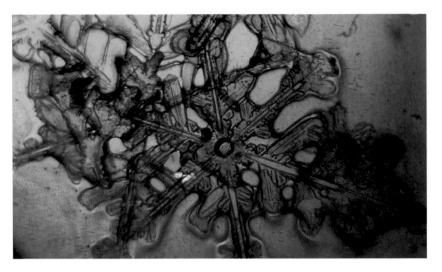

Above: Although "no two snowflakes are ever alike," all possess the same six-fold symmetry; that is, all have the same group property. In this case successive sixty-degree rotations around the crystal's short axis do not change the way the snowflake looks.

Right: The tetragonal symmetry modelled here belongs to several naturally occurring minerals, including tin and several kinds of silica. Crystallographers exhaust the possibilities in a classification scheme consisting of 32-point groups (rotations) and a much larger number of space groups (linear motions and reflections).

fundamental questions in mathematics. Poisson found it incomprehensible. Those parts Poisson understood, he (like Cauchy) ascribed to Abel without seeing how much farther and deeper Galois had gone. ("Poisson," Abel had once written, "is a little fellow; he knows how to behave with a great deal of dignity.")

Duel to the Death

Galois, now frustrated, made a quick failure of teaching his own public mathematics course. He joined a republican National Guard artillery regiment and was twice tried by the reactionary authorities in the aftermath of tumultuous demonstrations. He spent ten months in political detention in July 1831. Upon his release, he was challenged, in a provocation that was apparently planned, to a duel. In these desperate circumstances, he scribbled his last, testamentary letter, trying to draw attention to the meaning of his work, published only in fragments during the four-year blaze of his career. He died of a pistol wound inflicted the next morning. Thus, his most important findings were published posthumously.

What later mathematicians discovered in Galois's dispersed work is the foundation of what is known today as group theory, and, incidentally, a definitive solution to the problem of algebraic equations of fifth degree or higher. These and other deeply insightful results were not fully absorbed until the 1860s, when Serret and Jordan confidently took his methods forward. The group concept is elusive (ask Poisson) but illuminable. If Poisson had difficulty following Galois's ideas into higher levels, it is no wonder. Grouping things together just to see how many ways it can be done doesn't seem an especially relevant method for extracting deep mathematical truths, but it leads to some of the rarest insights in mathematics.

The Group Theory Contribution

To begin, according to Galois, a *group* isn't, mathematically speaking, just any collection of things that happen to be together. The group possesses an operation that can work on any two members at a time. Think of all the real numbers (0, 1, 2, 3, etc.) and, say, the operation of multiplication. The members and the operation make up the

group. There are a few more conditions to be met for grouphood, which multiplication of real numbers also happens to meet, namely: (1) Any time the operation is carried out, its result must also be in the group. Multiplying any two real numbers together always gives another real number. This suggests groups will always possess the property of dullness—the group operation never results in anything new or surprising. On the other hand, the operation's ability always to "reach" group members, and only group members, sets these elements aside as specially connected. With Galois's theorems, one may immediately infer certain qualities about groups in general and about particular groups, setting them apart from others.

(2) At least one operation must leave everything unchanged. Multiplying any real number by one doesn't change anything. One is called the *identity element* of this particular group. (3) Every member of the group must have an *inverse*, an opposite, so that putting the two together yields the identity element. Inverses "undo" each other, so to speak. Every real number has an inverse; multiplying the two (for example, 5 and $\frac{1}{5}$) is guaranteed to come out one. (4) You can string operations together: since the operation (multiplication) really only works on two things at a time, it doesn't matter if you perform, say, $2 \times 3 \times 4$ as 6×4 or 2×12.

High Abstraction

Curiously, groups *don't* require that 2×3 be the same as 3×2, or that $2 \times 3 \times 4$ equal $2 \times 4 \times 3$. Multiplication of real numbers does happen to have that property (called *commutivity*), but it just places the arithmetic of real numbers among what are known as Abelian groups.

Group theory would be crashingly trivial thinking if it did no more than add another paragraph to simple arithmetic. But the members of a group are in no way restricted, beyond the four basic qualities, to mere objects. The idea *is* very general—a piece of high abstraction.

A set of operations might be taken as the members of a group, like turning a sphere through a series of prescribed rotations, say, combining all 90-degree up or down rotations with 90-degree left or right spins. (It's performing two of these spin-maneuvers one after another that is the *group* operation.) Listing all possible combinations—left, right, up, down—gives sixteen distinct expressions. But an identity element is also needed, a spin of zero degrees, and a spin of 180° to round out the group, and give it all of the group properties. That makes six elements and a total of 36 combinations. This example is a bit of a relief because it is finite. Multiplication of real numbers, the first example, could never be written out. The group goes on as far as the real numbers, *i.e.* infinitely.

We might use a world globe to investigate the way groups work. For a compact illustration, confine the group "multiplication" table to just the left-right-up-down combinations. This is not the whole group, but it reaches all the permitted results. Starting each time at one place on the globe—Borneo will do—and carrying out the reduced set of 16 spin operations leads to five other locales on Earth, listed below with more or less geographic exactness:

GROUP MULTIPLICATION TABLE

Sdd = Brazil	Sdl = Jarvis I.	Sdr = Zaire	Sdu = Borneo
Sld = South Pole	Sll = Brazil	Slr = Borneo	Slu = North Pole
Srd = South Pole	Srl = Borneo	Srr = Brazil	Srd = N Pole
Sud = Borneo	Sul = Jarvis I.	Sur = Zaire	Suu = Brazil

S=spin, d=down, l=left, u=up, r=right

Group Representations

The important things to notice here are, first, the order of doing the operations matters—going down-left, for example, doesn't end up at the same place as left-down. Well, it *is* a group, so no surprise. Second, all the combined operations—they're transformations in the general sense—lead to only six outcomes. These six outcomes form a *representation* of the group. That anyone would look at this list of places on the globe and immediately think to tick off their group-theoretical implication isn't apt to happen. Nonetheless, reasoning backwards from a representation, a model of the group, to identify the group itself has its uses. This procedure has an important place in modern physics.

Notice, too, that there's no use looking for a seven- or a five-locale representation for this particular group—the group cannot come out that way. Groups often *do* have more than one representation—and there are ways of finding them—but any representation not on the list simply cannot occur.

Returning now to Galois and what group theory did for algebraic equations: Lagrange had realized that equations could be classified by the permutations possible on elements (coefficients of the x's, x^2's, etc.) making up their algebraic expressions, indeed that only certain sets of permutations necessarily lead to permissible values (like Borneo or Zaire). Permutations, moreover, can be carried out as a chain of substitutions, replacing one term with another, step by step, until all combinations have been exhausted. Though Lagrange didn't yet see it quite this way, permutations form *substitution groups*. (Substitution is just the defining group operation, instead of addition, multiplication, or rotation, or whatever.)

Abel and Ruffino carried the idea far enough to show the relevant permutations of the general quintic equation (*i.e.*, with x^5 in it) can't have the right numbers of group members for an all-purpose algebraic solution to be possible. (An algebraic solution can only use the ordinary operations of arithmetic and radicals.)

Galois broadened the whole study, to a consideration of substitution groups. He proved that every equation belongs to one, and only one, group and that the properties of the group say a great deal about whether the equation is soluble by algebraic methods—whether the group has representations that fit the globe, as it were, although it is a bit more complex. Every substitution group of four or fewer elements turns out to be completely soluble by algebra. In fact, Galois took groups into the realm of irrationals, beyond the formal limits of rational functions, casting new light on the nature of equations of fifth degree and greater.

The Symmetry Rabbit Trick

For the most part, group theory remained a remote, abstruse sort of mathematics until mid-twentieth century. Demonstrations by specialists seemed a bit magical—not like pulling a rabbit out of a hat exactly, but being able to prove from which hats a rabbit will come, without ever having seen the equipment. In the real world, crystallographers had profitably organized lattices into group memberships. The rest of physics had to go to school on groups after Germany's Emmy Noether proved in 1918 that some very important symmetries, which turn out to be laws of conservation, are enumerable through "Lie groups"—another miserably abstract kind of mathematizing. On the whole, one would rather just wait and watch for the rabbit.

Groups usually don't provide concrete solutions, just subtly complete descriptions. Insofar as physicists spend a lot of time trying to find what remains invariant in many kinds of processes—transfer of energy, moving about in a force field, or whatever—group theory brings the subject into sharp focus. The problem becomes one of discovering what kinds of changes, or transformations, end up in the same place. Or, what is an equivalent idea, how many symmetries there are in the possible outcomes and of what kind. Still, if it cleans up the thinking in quantum mechanics, that's not an advance to be sniffed at.

Oddly enough, physicists did begin materializing some solid group rabbits in the 1960s. By that time, discovering nuclear particles had become a frustrating success—they were everywhere, a new one in every new journal. One way of keeping track involves looking for symmetry groups among particle properties (quantum numbers). There had been hints before. Werner Heisenberg and Wolfgang Pauli had associated symmetries with some simpler pieces of the puzzle. And mathematicians had long since efficiently laid out all the possible transformation groups. The task of sorting through candidate groups looking for good fits finally paid off when Murray Gell-Mann determined in 1961 that a basic three-dimensional group, named SU(3), had a suitable eight-dimensional representation. It seemed to organize the eight baryons (certain heavy particles including protons and neutrons) and the eight mesons in a meaningful, if unexpected way. (Gell-Mann called his find the "eightfold way," recalling the Buddhist path to nirvana.)

Everything threatened to come apart soon thereafter because SU(3) didn't explain another set of nine short-lived "resonance" particles. There are no 9-dimensional representations in SU(3). After some thought, Gell-Mann predicted the existence of a tenth particle—SU(3) does have a 10-dimensional representation. With the discovery of the omega minus resonance, the tenth particle, group theory pulled its rabbit out of the hat. Only the first of many, as it turns out. Puzzlement over why no one had observed anything that might correspond to the basic, "defining" three-dimensional representation of SU(3), led to Gell-Mann's conjecturing quarks into existence. And the rest, as they say, is history.

Physics has moved on, looking for even more unifying symmetries—SU(5) has more theoretical literature than most—to explain at some level why the universe is composed of the particles and forces we find in it. The group mathematics hasn't gotten any easier, now running to such things as "gauge" symmetries, so that one can only hope, should the ultimate answers come, they will belong to a group that possesses a representation in clear words.

Above: *Physicists inferred the existence of quarks purely through group theory (with the aid of brute computer power). Physical evidence supporting their theoretical constructs only emerged in the 1990s in the form of bubble chamber photos like this one, which shows distinctive tracks of condensation in the wake of passing particles. Some may find the "evidence" scant clarification of the already abstruse theory of Gell-Mann and fellow investigators.*

Johann Gregor Mendel [1822-84]

There is a particular scientific method, extremely useful and not terribly abstract, that scarcely appeared anywhere before the late nineteenth century. The power tools of mathematics—like differential equations, matrix operations, group theory—can accomplish a great deal where a few basic, component relationships have already been built. In the case of electromagnetism, for example, laws pertaining to charge, current, resistance, and induction (bearing the names of their discoverers, Coulomb, Ampère, Ohm, and Faraday) define some endpoints that the larger generalization of Maxwell's field equations must also arrive at. Maxwell's equations, in turn, delimited the forms that Einstein could consider in working toward an even more inclusive description: special relativity. What the heavy mathematical equipment won't do is furnish those fundamental descriptions that someone has to come up with in the first place. This is the business of experiment, usually conducted with an array of scientific equipment and arriving at measurable results. But some areas of knowledge—such as the actuarial tables used by insurance companies—are built from a kind of "experiment" that simply relies on finding a numerical pattern in past events. The method is *statistical*.

A New Kind of Experiment

Among the very first to perceive the utility of searching for scientific facts with statistics is Gregor Mendel. The enormous body of his experiment, cultivation of nearly 30,000 plants, simply overwhelmed the underlying lack of a good mechanical model in genetics. No one in 1860—Mendel included—had the slightest notion of what chromosomes look like or how they are redistributed in reproduction. Mendel only intended to show that something very like a gene, an "element" as he called it, must be responsible for the heritability of traits.

Right: Chromosomes, as seen through a high-power microscope. Every living cell in the human body (except for reproductive cells) contains a full forty-six of them. Mendel deduced that some such biochemical units must be responsible for the genetically directed growth of all organisms.

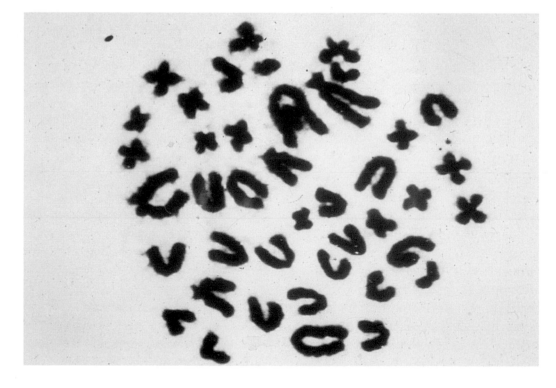

Mendel came from a farming family in the Silesian border area of what is now the Czech Republic but was then part of the Austro-Hungarian empire. Near the end of his schooling, in his sixteenth year, a serious accident took his father out of farming. In need of a living, Mendel tried tutoring. The pressure was too much: his health broke, and he spent some time recuperating before continuing his education. In fact, he never handled stress well. Preparing for crucial exams on two later occasions, he broke down. Not that he was in any way stunted for having blown the finals; he absorbed a great deal in attendance at the universities of Olmutz and Vienna, studying subjects such as combinatorial analysis, physics, botany, plant physiology, and chemistry under notable professors.

The troublesome exams were those needed for a secondary-level teaching certificate. (He was accounted an excellent teacher, albeit officially a substitute teacher, by his later colleagues and students.) He seems to have been shy, sensitive, easily reduced to a depressive state by untoward events. His second stay at Olmutz—the first ended in a finance-induced breakdown—was partly paid for by his younger sister, from her dowry, and resulted in a recommendation by his physics professor for admission to the Augustinian monastery at Brno. Though this sounds a bit odd today, especially since Mendel had no strong religious leanings, it was an inspired idea. The monastery had a lively, uncloistered involvement in the sciences, provided excellent teachers to the region, and often sent brothers off for advanced studies.

Below: Mendel, a reflective, quiet scientist, sent off his chief discoveries to a few distinguished professors, but they went unnoticed or unappreciated until thirty-five years after publication.

The evenness of life at Brno and freedom from financial worry worked wonderfully on Mendel's state of mind. After completing the usual courses in theology and several years at the University of Vienna, in 1856 he began his own scientific investigations. One is familiar, the initial pea plantings, and the other perhaps less well known. He began systematically recording and compiling weather data at Brno. (The papers containing his meteorological observations slightly outnumber those he produced on genetics.) Indeed, his influence helped to inaugurate, in the Moravian region, the first weather forecasts for farmers.

The Nature of Heredity

The monks at Brno often had several botanical trials going; Mendel himself was active in various societies for promoting and improving agriculture. When he was elected abbott of the monastery, in 1868, he succeeded F. C. Napp, another energetic agriculturalist. The position was to prove onerous: a Liberal government of the 1870s forced contributions from the religious estate; though a long-standing Liberal supporter, Mendel felt duty-bound to resist. A long, intermittent struggle with the authorities took a predictable toll on his health and certainly hastened his death.

In life he created few scientific ripples. The results he published, the very foundation of modern genetics, resembled cursorily the hybridization catalogs of Linnaeus, Koelreuter, and Gaertner, to name but a few of the leading experimentalists. An extensive knowledge already existed in the method of generating crosses along with a good deal of unquantified opinion about tendencies in one species or another. To his contemporaries, the worthy monk's pea plants just looked like another solid little contribution to better agriculture. And it's not in the nature of quiet genius, or of monks for that matter, to clamor for recognition.

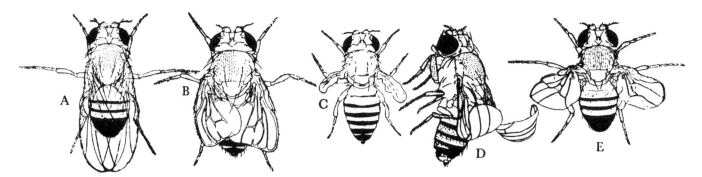

It hadn't occurred to anyone before Mendel (even after Darwin had become commonplace) that an experiment could be designed to test the intrinsic nature of inheritance. Perhaps it would have made a difference if Mendel had deliberately brought scientists' attention to the new methodology he adopted, one particularly suited to the natural sciences. But this is in the nature of statistics; it really does just look like another few thousand pea plants until the terms of the experiment are understood. To begin, Mendel had sifted the literature for the most suitable, the stablest, candidate species for his experiment. Once *Pisum sativum*, the common pea, had been selected, he checked each strain's purity by growing a few generations of the plant. (The further stages of breeding were arduous, requiring manual cross-pollination of individual plants.)

Satisfied as to the reliability of his materials, Mendel crossed several easily verified traits in pairs, *e.g.,* a round seed strain with a wrinkled seed strain, yellow seed with green seed, purple-flowered with white-flowered. His aims were admirably precise—the basis that makes them scientifically testable and so unlike apparently similar undertakings. Pairs were crossed in isolation, to detect what rules of heritability might be operating, and crossed multiply, to ascertain any degree of interdependence among pairs of traits. In this he had brilliantly reduced an amorphously large realm to its kernel and formulated the key hypothesis as well, namely that traits are passed on as discrete, separable qualities. Thus, whatever the cause, whatever the exact form of the as yet unknown heritability "elements," the elements too would seem to be physically discrete and separable.

Most of the world, including the scientific world, still spoke vaguely about characteristics being acquired "in the blood," with a goodly use of "mingling" when it came down to describing the transfer. Mendel belonged to a more advanced circle, among whom a material "germ" was presumed to carry the inheritance, and by sexual means. He was aware of and endorsed, with a few scientific reservations, Darwin's view of the development of species. His own work, unfortunately, never came to the attention of Darwin.

In designing his experiments, Mendel managed to avoid stepping into a few of the soft places in this new science (though he could scarcely have known it); perhaps it was just good scientific instinct. For one thing, the traits he chose happen to be determined at a single gene location, so that crossing pairs unambiguously matches up the expression of two variant forms of a single gene. (These variant forms are now called *alleles*.) Highly distinct traits, those with no known "shadings" between them, usually fall into the single-gene class. For another, the pea isn't much of a polymorph: it isn't genetically saturated with so many alleles that picking out useful marker traits becomes quite difficult. Mendel encountered trouble on this score in some subsequent trials with hawkweed.

***Above:** Mendel hoped to breed a new "synthetic race" from among fifty bee varieties he hybridized. He could find no satisfactory means of controlling fertilization of the queen bees, however.*

Above: The monastery at Brno—now a museum dedicated to Mendel—and a patch of its garden. The flowerbed demonstrates the ratio of occurrence of the color red (the dominant trait) to white (the recessive trait) in successive generations of the flower. Many plant breeding and growth projects were undertaken in Mendel's day, with the aim of improving farming in the region. Lively controversies occasionally flared among the agronomist monks, as well: one was dismissed for persisting in dubious Hegelian views on plant development.

What Mendel observed in the first two generations of crossbred *Pisum* confirmed a pattern anticipated in his hypothesis. That pattern, by the way, he obtained by doing what any genius in his situation would do, he *counted* the traits produced; previous work abounded in qualitative description, but with few useful numbers attached. Mendel's first generation of offspring showed only one of the parent traits. The second generation mixed them in the proportion three to one. Well, very close to three to one; experiments should attract suspicion when the results come in neat integers. His actual count for the seed-shape trait was 5,474 round to 1,850 wrinkled, or 2.96 to 1. Other traits fell in the range 2.84 to 3.15 to one.

The Law of Segregation

This picture, according to Mendel, is most simply explained by assuming each parent donates a single factor, so that two are present in the offspring. The factors do not blend into each other producing, say, a pastel flower instead of purple or white, rather one of them, the *dominant* trait, is expressed. The remaining trait, *recessive*, may be present, but it cannot show unless an offspring has received two of the recessive element. What we now know, but Mendel did not, is that information to build any living species is transmitted in its chromosomes—long, twisted strands of DNA—whose lengths are marked out in biochemical segments, each making up a single gene. (Finding where one gene ends and the next begins and what exactly each does is an immense challenge to science today.)

We now know that chromosomes happen to come in pairs—twenty-three of them in humans, for example, where the chromosome expressing sex is an unlike pair in males. In reproduction, chromosome pairs are remixed, so to speak, in a random way. Only one of each chromosome is carried in any germ cell (*e.g.*, sperm or ovum), so that when two germ cells combine, a new set of chromosome pairs is created. *Two* copies of every gene, two alleles, thus are always present in the complete chromosome complement. Any two alleles may in fact be identical, *homozygous*, or somewhat different, *heterozygous*; it all depends on what assortments were available in the germ cells.

Mendel had got it right. When he looked at the first generation, he expected to find only one trait expressed, because the purity of his original strains insured that each parent had a like pair of alleles. That is, in the case of flower colors for example, purple parents contribute chromosomes with like color genes, *PP* (*P* for purple, capitalized for dominance). White parents donate *ww*. Every first-generation descendant, therefore, inherits *Pw* and turns out purple, since *w* is recessive. The second generation, however, is parented by the mixed-gene population, all of them *Pw*'s. A simple permutation gives four equally likely outcomes:

$$PP \quad Pw \quad wP \quad ww$$

Of these pairings only *ww* will show as a white flower, hence the observed ratio of three purple to one white bloom. This genetic way of rolling the dice was enunciated by Mendel as the law of segregation, *i.e.,* of the unitary, separate nature of the elements that pass on particular traits.

Taking the idea a generation or two further, he showed that *ww*'s, the only white flowers in the second generation, produce nothing but white flowers in succeeding offspring, if allowed to breed true. No unaccounted variable emerges. The purple plants, though, still possess among themselves like (homozygous) and unlike (heterozygous) pairings of alleles in the color-gene location. They continued to bring forth purple and white offspring in a predictable ratio. Mendel left very little room for doubt.

The Law of Independent Assortment

The proof is strengthened by crossing several different traits at once—Mendel worked up to seven—and looking once again for a chance distribution in the way traits are thrown together, which will occur only if individual elements don't combine or influence each other in any way. Writing out the permutation is a little longer, but his multi-trait plants turned up in good agreement with the calculated frequencies. The results confirm a second dictum, Mendel's law of independent assortment.

Later series of experiments, with bees and with other plant species, never achieved quite the same clarity as the *Pisum* trials. Not that his principles of hybridization were ever put in doubt, but some assortments of genes can mask or mimic others in the expression of seemingly distinct traits. Remarkably, he inferred some of these phenomena from his data, but hadn't the opportunity to investigate in greater detail. Sorting it all out was left to Mendel's successors, the first of whom didn't arrive until 1900, about thirty years late. They arrived all in a bunch, as a matter of fact. Hugo de Vries, Carl Correns, and Erik Tschermak, all working independently, obtained similar genetic rules, and just before publishing—within two months of one another—each discovered and reported Mendel's considerable priority in the field.

Below: With the aid of principles discovered by Gregor Mendel and his successors, plant and animal traits have been selectively bred—or even directly altered to improve agricultural efficiency.

Blundering Around with Genetics

There are any number of ways to make running guesses about how traits *could* be inherited—not even a particularly taxing exercise for an imaginative species like ourselves. Through the centuries, however, a few basic notions often recur. Two-and-a-half thousand years ago Aristotle would have the world believe that offspring acquired parts of their nature from every male that ever mated with the mother. A belief in telegony, as it's sometimes called, persists even now in places, though it seems more evidentially apt to describe our inheritance of superstitions.

Other durable misconceptions concern prenatal influences, the idea that genetic make-up of the unborn is susceptible to formative change by events outside the womb. The truth is otherwise, fortunately, else expectant mothers might bring about lamentable breaches of development through inadvertence in, say, reading habits. Not that the prenatal environment isn't chancy enough, with many unknowns, but genes assemble themselves without regard at least to literary taste.

Most tenacious of pre-Mendelian concepts, however, is the proposition that characteristics acquired in life may be passed along in the genes. Though the theory has existed in many forms, it's often called Lamarckism, after Jean-Baptiste Lamarck (1744–1829) its most distinguished expositor. Lamarck held, in a famous example, that giraffes acquired long necks through generations of stretching for ever higher foliage. This means that an alteration or special development of the bodily form, the *phenotype*, works somehow to direct future generations' genes, the *genotype*. A Darwinian, by contrast, would hold that long necks evolve by preferential survival of some giraffe progenitors with randomly variant genes which happen to express slightly longer necks. The process of getting to really long necks takes a lot of changes, most of which probably didn't work very well, and those producing most-likely-to-succeed giraffes

Right: Twins have always been in demand for genetic studies; they're a natural starting point for investigating the separate contributions of genes and environment—nature vs. nurture—to development. Results, however, are seldom so clear-cut as scientists might wish (and were even faked in several now infamous papers by Cyril Burt, a leading English authority in the 1940s and '50s).

Left: The view of Lamarck and others that giraffes, for example, regulate genetic change through will or behavior (like acquiring long necks by questing for high foliage) is intuitively appealing but a scientific dead end. Chromosomes, pure chance, and natural selection make a more convincing giraffe.

obviously come to predominate in the genotype—other genotypes, on the whole, arriving at extinction.

No evidence for phenotypic influence has come to light. Lamarck, with a brilliant, ranging intellect, might have changed his mind if he'd had a chance to read Mendel or Darwin. Or maybe not; he was eclectic and somewhat contrary by nature. He performed definitive taxonomic studies on invertebrates, virtually created the modern science museum, and gave biology its name. But he much preferred a grand sweep in theories and clashed with some of the best science of his own day. A modern reader coming across his *Zoological Philosophy* would likely take the title to mean approximately "a way to think about zoology"—which doesn't seem especially inspiring—whereas Lamarck probably intended something more along

the lines of "a way to think *up* zoology."

Such pursuits aren't confined to slightly *outré* eighteenth-century generalists; much that is unscientific can be pressed into ready-made ideological molds. Trofim Lysenko forced a varietal of neo-Lamarckism onto Soviet biology for about twenty-five years, from 1938 to 1963. The Lysenkoist position was found most consistent by Stalinist interpreters with the theories of Marx, though how the scholarly economist should have any bearing on genetics is quite inexplicable. Anyway, the development and teaching of genetics in Russia was greatly hampered. Hacks turned out hundreds of papers in support, and better scientists had to juggle with public and private versions of the subject until the key phenotype, Stalin, actually died without passing on this acquired mistake.

Robert Koch (1843-1910)

Koch once observed, toward the end of his life, that if he had achieved more than most in medicine, it was because he "came upon regions where gold was still lying by the wayside." His method had nothing to do with stumbling onto alluvial deposits; his modesty had a distinctly rhetorical ring. The understanding of disease had arrived at many confusing crossroads during the span of Koch's career. Important new knowledge lay in every direction, but it took rare energy and grasp to explore as much and as thoroughly as he did. The problems of physiology are never so clear as those in physics or mathematics. Koch had to make his own way, not only through the maze of nascent bacteriology but through a new world of science. He was the first of a thoroughly modern sort of investigator: well-grounded in several fields, able to define broad, long-range objectives, to assemble and direct research teams, and to make full use of rapidly developing technological means.

Wide-Ranging Interests

Born into a third-generation family of German mining officials in Klausthal, Hanover, Koch was fortunate in having a father who encouraged him in other directions. He manifested in childhood an industrious curiosity, collecting and studying plants, insects, and fossils, and preparing skeletons of larger animals. Later, at the University of Göttingen, he concentrated in medicine only after convincing himself that such a career would be highly compatible with his continuing interest in the natural sciences. The eminent faculty at the time included Jacob Henle, originator of the scientific germ theory of disease—though he never lectured on the subject, being a professor of anatomy. Association with Henle and his writings put Koch on the right track in the debate then raging in academic circles over miasmic versus microbial origin and contagion of disease. For that matter, it still wasn't settled to everyone's satisfaction that microbes weren't somehow "spontaneously generated" from inert substances or reassembly of dead organic parts. Not until 1866 did Pasteur begin the experiments that ruled out any spontaneous mechanism.

Koch demonstrated remarkable capacity for independent research and graduated in 1866 with highest distinction. He took the prize in a problem set by Henle to find and trace the distribution of uterine nerve ganglia and submitted, for his doctoral dissertation, original work on succinic acid production in the body. (He acted as his own guinea pig, putting away unpleasantly large amounts of various foods as required at successive stages of his investigation.) Although he always maintained that the confinement of an academic career was unappealing—and he loved to travel—the six years following his graduation were perhaps more unsettled than even he could wish. From 1866 to 1872 he practiced at several hospitals and privately in four East Prussian towns, as well as volunteering for medical service in the Franco-Prussian War.

Breakthroughs in Bacterial Research

Married by now and with a young daughter, Koch came to rest finally as district medical officer at Wollstein. Here, in a curtained-off laboratory, he began the researches that produced, by his own techniques, the first high-quality photomicrographs of bacteria, detailed by staining methods he developed. In 1876 he published his findings on the etiology of anthrax (an infectious disease), which represented a substantial advance over earlier approaches in that he appreciated a need

to observe bacteria over a controlled range of environmental conditions, selectively altering temperature, moisture, and oxygen supply. He was the first to report spore-forming and germination behavior in anthrax—which disclosed new routes of contagion.

With the publication of his next paper, on wound infections, he laid down what came to be called "Koch's postulates," the necessary and sufficient conditions for identifying a causative agent in disease; they are the ground rules of etiology. Though restated by him from time to time, his essential requirements are: (1) that the suspect microbes be detected in all cases of a disease under investigation; (2) that the microbes be isolated and grown in pure cultures; (3) that inoculation of test animals produce the disease with all its symptoms; (4) that the same microbe is recovered from diseased test animals.

It must be said that Koch was ambitious to get on with work at the pace and level

Below: The English surgeon Joseph Lister wholly accepted Pasteur's theory of germ contagion and operated, after about 1865, with a sterilizing carbolic acid spray in the area of an incision or wound. His procedure was deemed valuable, though many in the profession were not yet convinced of a bacterial role in infection.

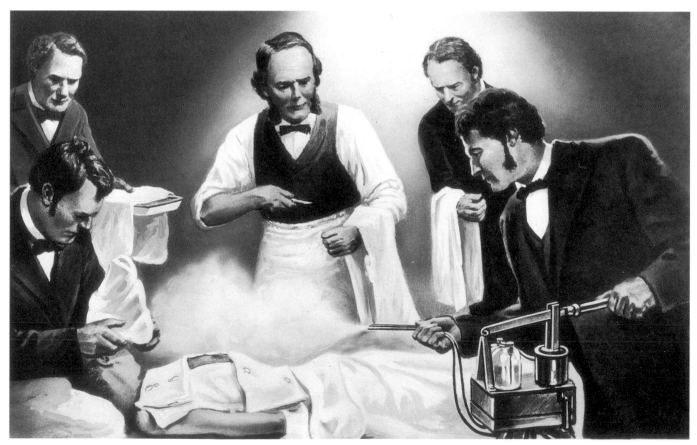

Above: Koch in his element in 1896, at a South African field laboratory, laboring to isolate the virus responsible for rinderpest.

he knew to be possible and was by no means averse to recognition for his efforts. That recognition came quickly, as did government-sponsored opportunities to set up laboratories. At his first facility, in a Berlin apartment house, he brought together assistants of high caliber, all of whom went on to distinguished careers.

In the eyes of the government, it was enough that Koch redounded to the national glory: the late nineteenth century construed every advance as another leg-up in a great patriotic race. Koch participated, certainly, in such enthusiasms; he had an almost military habit of command, with a quite military intolerance of criticism, especially from abroad. All the maneuverings for national prestige, in this context at least, intensified medical progress.

The Importance of Methodology

In a classic 1881 article on disease-causing agents, or *pathogens*, Koch set out a detailed method for laboratory studies. The aims of research must extend to discovery of a micro-organism's natural habitat, its sites of entry and localization within a host, its ability to cross-infect species, and to substances potentially active against the pathogen. Sterile technique was stressed above all, at every stage of the work. Cultures were to be grown in a solid medium (gelatin at first, replaced later by agar, compounded from marine algae) so that species and strains could not mingle, thereby confusing the result.

The value of an impeccable methodology was borne out in an Egyptian cholera outbreak of 1883. On the strength of Pasteur's announcement that cholera could reach Europe, French and German teams were despatched in the hope of characterizing both a cause and a treatment for

the disease. The French were still using Pasteur's method of culturing specimens in bouillon, and obtained teeming populations of intestinal bacteria. Koch, meanwhile, had isolated and grown in agar the previously unseen comma-shaped bacillus *Vibrio cholerae*, although he wasn't able to link it to the disease definitively until the following year, during an outbreak in India. He also demonstrated its presence in impure water supplies, with obvious implications for controlling the disease.

Koch was indefatigable in the service of medicine. In almost any year between 1883 and 1908, he could be found in a rough field laboratory somewhere in Africa, India, or the southwestern Pacific. (His pace wore out his first marriage; he remarried, an actress thirty years his junior, in 1893.) Throughout his hazardous, eventful life,

Above: *Only somewhat fanciful is this nineteenth-century Viennese attempt to ward off plague and cholera: herb-filled pockets, healthful infusions, and unamused companion.*

Left: *Modern protective attire for sterile lab conditions is a good deal less stylish but more effective.*

Above: *Governments quickly provided the means to carry forward the pioneering research. At the Pasteur Institute in Paris, scientists prepare a tetanus antitoxin.*

he continued to prepare lecture courses and co-edit the influential journal *Zeitschrift für Hygiene*. Even after his announced retirement at the age of sixty, and a Nobel Prize in 1905, he went to the Sudan, hot on the trail of a spirochete that he tied to African relapsing fever. The kaiser saw fit, from time to time, to pin another medal on his chest or to elevate his state rank, bestowing eventually upon him the grand-sounding *Wirklicher Geheimer Rat*, with claim to the honorific *Excellenz*.

The researchers he led identified bacterial or protozoan causative agents in diphtheria (Loeffler), typhoid (Gaffky), variant forms of trypanosomiasis (sleeping sickness), and a host of animal diseases. Koch himself devoted years to the understanding of malaria, characterizing its vector transmission (by mosquitoes),

control measures (drainage), and therapeutic regimen (quinine is toxic unless reliably prepared and administered). Occasionally, even in studying diseases in which no bacterium could be implicated (caused by viruses, as yet undiscovered), adherence to Koch's meticulous procedures enabled preparation of vaccines from laboratory isolates. At the facilities he established, with government funding, at Göttingen and Berlin, the best minds of his generation and the next worked or trained; the distinguished corps includes Nobel laureates Paul Ehrlich and Emil von Behring.

The Struggle Against Tuberculosis

Running through Koch's entire career is a stubborn struggle toward a treatment for tuberculosis. He'd found the cause, an especially small bacillus resistant to staining, in 1882; prior to his epochal papers on the subject, a large body of medical opinion held that the symptoms arose by a degenerative process, related variously to miasmas or individual constitution. Koch seems to have expected, however, that *Mycobacterium tuberculosis* might yield quickly to the usual vaccine trials. He announced prematurely, in 1890, that he'd prepared an inhibitory substance, tuberculin, effective in controlling the disease. Like the news of a miracle drug today, the event precipitated a controversy over control of its manufacture, how much of the formula to reveal, and cost to patients.

At first, Koch resisted disclosing tuberculin's makeup (it is a bacillary concentrate in glycerine), but he provided details as it became clear that therapeutic trials weren't reporting the successes he had hoped for. The original tuberculin and modifications had some effect, but with significant risks, against the disease in its earliest stages; the substance proved more useful in diagnosis (the patch test). During intervals between more pressing investigations, Koch worked on the control of tuberculosis for the rest of his life. In 1908, the same year in which the first Koch Medal was awarded (to Koch), a group of wealthy donors—among them Andrew Carnegie and Kaiser Wilhelm II— endowed a Koch Foundation for the study of tuberculosis. If Koch never disposed of the tubercule bacillus in the way he had hoped, it's because he matched himself against a tenacious adversary; tuberculosis has only been treatable from the mid-twentieth century, and new strains show every indication of resistance to current therapy. But as Koch undoubtedly would say, and as he constantly exhorted his colleagues, *Nicht locker lassen!*—"Don't let up!"

Left: *A bacteriologist's dream: antibiotics. Penicillin cultures are being evaluated for effectiveness against disease-causing strains.*

Immunity and Pasteur

Right: *Pasteur in his lab, with animal subjects in serum trials.*

Below: *Louis Pasteur firmly established the cause of infection as living, identifiable microbes.*

Although the name of Louis Pasteur has come to be associated first in the public mind with conquering disease, he came rather late to research in bacteriology, undertaking his famous work on anthrax at the age of fifty-five. The fact that he was a brilliant physicist and chemist—the discoverer of "handedness" in otherwise identical molecules—tends to become sub-

merged in his later achievements. His views on disease were certainly in keeping with the best science: he read the papers of Lister, Koch, and Ehrlich with the same attention that they read his. However, Pasteur arrived by a different route.

One of Pasteur's early specializations as a chemist led him to a long study of the fermentation process, a topic of national import in France. Systematically elucidating the role of live yeast in the manufacture of alcohol, he demolished the notion of spontaneous generation and the eminent von Leibig's view that alcohol precipitates chemically from the products of decomposed yeast. Without addressing himself, as yet, to characterizing any particular microbe, he had shown by the early 1860s that some thrived in air, while others took oxygen from compounds in their preferred environments.

With or without von Leibig, fermentation is not an unalloyed blessing; continued biological activity can, for example, sour wine. Aware that living organisms are required for this baneful result, Pasteur sought a controlled heat treatment to eliminate the organisms while preserving the wine. The result, "pasteurization," was available in 1865. (Only later was it used for milk.) Had Koch explored parallel routes, the comparison might have been memorable. Both men were intensely nationalistic, both authoritarian by nature—Pasteur was seldom put in charge of anything after a brief reign at the Ecole Normale—and by the 1870s Pasteur was considering a vexing problem: why were German beers so good, and French beers, well, French?

Not even Pasteur had a satisfactory answer to the question, but reflection on the processes at work convinced him that biological agents are no less capable of growth and activity in animals and man than in beer, wine, or milk. Thus in 1876, with a career already behind him that any scientist could envy, and still paralyzed on his left side by a stroke suffered eight years earlier, Pasteur at last set out toward his discoveries of anthrax and rabies vaccines (and, indeed, the whole concept of attenuated vaccines), and toward the expression, with Emile Roux, of a chemical theory of immunity.

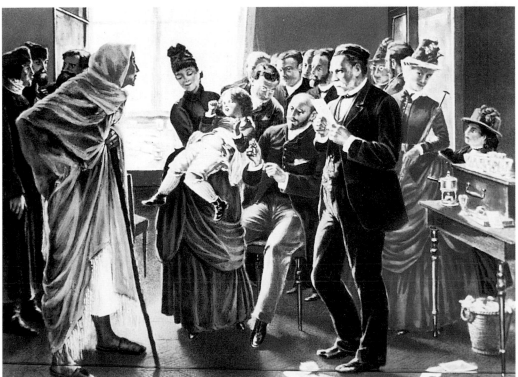

Above: *The forward march of medicine was infused with the intense patriotic spirit of the late nineteenth century. Pasteur, wreathed in tricolor, was no less a national hero in France than Koch in Germany.*

Left: *A child being vaccinated at Pasteur's laboratory. The products of the new research were rapidly available and proved, perhaps for the first time in medicine's history, dramatically beneficial.*

Ivan Pavlov [1849-1936]

***Above:** Pavlov explored a difficult science at the boundary of biochemisty and behavior. From his now classic experiments in the relation of behavior to environment, he drew structural clues to the working of the brain.*

Whereas the centuries since Newton had delved the physical universe, discussion generally turned philosophical when scientists intruded into the proprietary matters of life: will and idea, desire, reason, and so on. Qualitative terms really aren't manageable in science. Darwin and the evolutionists—the careful ones, at any rate—were never so brash as to propose natural selection of the spirit, though they tried heartily enough to equate survival with moral sense, culture, and social fitness.

Early psychologists—including Freud—threw out old vocabularies and invented new psychoanalytic terms with meanings that seemed to shift uncomfortably. Frames of reference wouldn't stay nailed down and many suspected that in this area "science" was being loosely used. Someone needed to put forth a clear language of experiment—Ivan Pavlov, for one, took on this task.

Physiology Meets Psychology

He was born in the ancient Russian town of Ryazan to the family of a priest. His early education in religious schools didn't deprive him of the opportunity to keep up with his real interests in natural science. In 1870 he departed the Ryazan seminary in midcourse to concentrate on scientific studies at the University of St. Petersburg. He graduated with distinction, already a promising researcher in physiology. After enrolling at the Imperial Medical Academy, further work resulted in a medical degree and laboratory association with leading experimentalists, including S.P. Botkin, whose integrated view of the nervous system deeply influenced Pavlov's thinking.

Pavlov finished off the academic rounds with a doctoral dissertation—on efferent nerves of the heart—and a two-year working tour of the German laboratories of Karl Ludwig and Rudolf Heidenhain. In 1881 he married another student, Serafima Karchevskaya, a friend of Fyodor Dostoyevsky. It's perhaps the most impulsive thing he ever did; they had to live apart for a while because of his impoverished student circumstances. He was otherwise a colossus of routine, who showed up at his laboratory punctually each morning—even while a revolution surged in the streets. With fairly smooth advancement to a professor's standing at the Imperial Academy by 1890 and various departmental appointments, insolvency ceased to be as constant an annoyance. In later years, after the Bolsheviks took power, he refused any special comforts not offered to his colleagues.

Broadly speaking, Pavlov's physiological career developed in three often overlapping phases: investigation of the heart and circulation, the activities of digestion, and complex nervous function and the brain. (His 1904 Nobel Prize specifically recognized work on the digestive system.) That a mere scalpel-wielder should come to rearrange the fundamental understanding of human behavior was unthinkable. But from the outset Pavlov made it clear he wasn't interested in simple test-tube research that catches, say, an individual enzyme in the act. His physiology needed to understand the whole organism at work. To this end his thinking, and thus his experiments, treated the living entity as a complex of activities—neurally interconnected, to be sure, and often grouped within specific organs.

Inherent in his approach, the jumping-off place into a new science (or several of them) is the notion that objective inquiry, with patient synthesis of discrete physical findings, can hope to discover the nature of the subjective: experience, emotion, learning, personality. Pavlov carried his program to scientific maturity, opening up the neurological pathways of behavior and the role of environmental stimuli.

As to the methodology of the scalpel, we are understandably queasy today. Indeed, it's hard to know in the history of medicine which events are excesses and which are merely nauseating. The experimental use of animals, without anesthesia at that, raises ethical concern. A difference of eras and outlooks does some injustice to Pavlov, who insisted on standards of operating-room practice and recuperative care often unavailable, ironically enough, to human patients of his time. He was extraordinarily deft with his instruments; he tolerated no sloppy or crude work.

In the Laboratory

It would only occur to a physiologist to study the brain by looking at salivary glands. That was Pavlov's intent in the famous series of experiments with dogs, metronomes, buzzers, and such. He'd already noticed seemingly unprompted salivation in dogs; it seemed reasonable the brain had made a mistake or was directing other behavior into which the instruction to sali-

Below: Pavlov's lab at the Institute of Experimental Medicine swelled at times to three hundred researchers and numerous subject species, from fish to mammals. Gifted students added physiological perspective to fields such as psychology, genetics, and evolution. Pavlov administered the establishment quite ably, while still prodigiously active in experiment and theory.

Above: The high caliber of Pavlov's work and his incorruptible standards inspired two generations of Russian scientists. In the Academy of Sciences, voting as a minority of one, he refused to countenance the Stalinist politicization of professorships.

by contrast, belongs to a different class. Dogs invariably salivate when it's offered—an example of what Pavlov called an unconditional stimulus. Should the metronome sound just before the meat arrives, becoming associated with it, the test subject will soon begin to salivate whenever the ticking is heard. The metronome, then, ceases to be neutral and becomes a *conditioned* stimulus; the dog, which is now said to be *sensitized* to the metronome, has learned a *conditioned* behavior, it has a *conditioned reflex* linking metronome and meat. (The terms first appear in his writings in 1903.)

Actually, Pavlov said (in Russian) that the dog picks up a "conditional" reflex, emphasizing the temporarily altered effect of the once neutral metronome on behavior. "Conditioned" reflex, as it's always translated, seems to connote more a training process. Probably not what Pavlov had in mind, but close enough. Either way it points to new connections, which must be neurochemical, being made in the brain. The ability to extinguish such a connection, by withholding meat, proved to Pavlov the alterable, adaptive nature of brain connections.

Measures of Behavior

Demonstrating the big idea rarely qualifies by itself as good science. "The devil is in the details," and so is the real shape of behavior. Pavlov and others set about to determine the behavioral equivalents of strength and distance: how much stimulus, how many competing stimuli, how long to sensitize, how long to extinguish, and so forth. This also led to discovering what *isn't* a stimulus: when he couldn't condition dogs to color differences, he concluded they are color blind.

Successful animals, like ourselves, can learn which stimuli are the best forecasters among many of an impending meat delivery, how to influence its likelihood, or how quickly to abandon expectation. If

vate had been swept up. Theorists of the subjective school would maintain the dog had simply made a wish to receive some good food. That seemed rather arbitrary to Pavlov, not at all tied in to the kinds of reflexive patterns he'd dealt with at every level of body systems. His assumption, at any rate, is that the brain puts behavior together in some consistent ways while interacting with its environment.

To begin, Pavlov first tested the effect of a metronome alone on a dog's physiological state. It had none; the metronome is a neutral stimulus, a fine example of the thousand things in an environment that evoke no inborn response. Powdered meat,

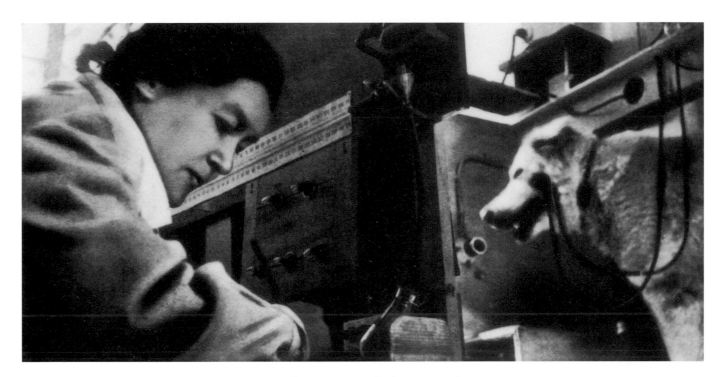

our capacity is overstrained, overstimulated and under-rewarded, we may damage the learning gear.

For Pavlov these insights led naturally to the investigation of badly made adaptations to stimulus: he induced neurotic behavior in test subjects with the same means, applied differently. How else to explain a phobia, say, a fear of round objects, other than by conditioning?

Certain round objects might come into view just before a painful event. The object of the phobia is, in the usual case, a neutral stimulus; only association of the object, Pavlov reasoned, with a far more powerful unconditioned stimulus could account for phobic behavior. More complicated disruption, too, is possible by saturating an environment with random, indecipherable cues—with no way to predict or

Above and below:
Observation underway with dogs at the Pavlov Institute. Pavlov demanded a high level of care for the animals, who spent their entire lives at the Institute.

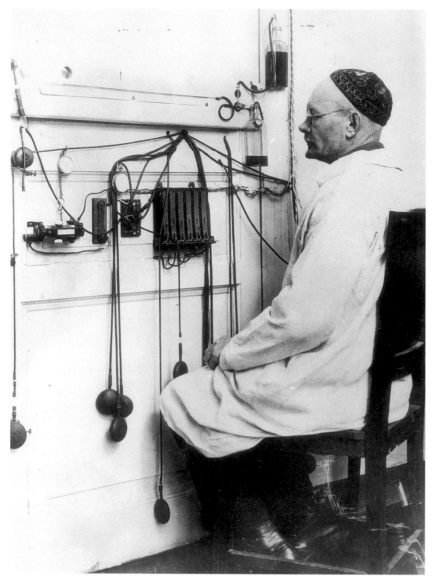

that anything so intricate as a human being can be "reduced" to simple mechanisms. In the present era, discoveries in genetics and artificial intelligence appear to encroach in the same way that Darwin and Pavlov's theories affected their own times. Pavlov estimated the underlying state of affairs to be anything but simple; the tangle of associations constantly being made and tested in the brain, its sheer capacity to integrate so much information, is daunting. That Pavlov placed too much reliance on a single means of describing behavior—the conditioned reflex—is true, but only subsequent experiment could make that clear.

All theories tend to inflate themselves at every hint of breakthrough, inferring too much, too fast. Well-founded criticism deflates them just as quickly. The general result in psychology has been that larger schemes must answer first to behavioral findings and at least interpret them before proceeding. As to fretting over that indefinable specialness of being conscious, thinking animals: this high-minded level of objection, regardless of validity, seems hardly to the point in a world that's already put "operant conditioning," "behavioral modification," and other textbook manipulation into routine commercial and political use.

Unhappily, Pavlov was to spend the last twenty years of his life in tenacious resistance to an ideological program which frankly enlisted psychology in its political method—not a pretty compliment to the success of his scientific views. For the sake of the social experiment that was communism, he said in 1923, he "would not sacrifice a frog's hind legs." He often found himself in a noisy minority of one, speaking his mind in defense of the aims of science in a way that living voices seldom dared. His stature somehow preserved him to the very end, still wrangling with commissars and the mysteries of behavior.

Above: *It's reasonable to wonder whose behavior is being observed here—the scientist or the animal subject on the other side of the Pavlov Institute's experiment door. Such bell-and-whistle apparatus has colored behavioral studies with a sense of mechanical determinacy. Pavlov held, more broadly, that behavior arises through the interaction of many processes, conditioned reflexes among them.*

avoid disappointment. Normal behavior may break down across a broad front. A dog conditioned, for example, to discriminate between perfect circles and ovals explodes with frustration when the ovals become so nearly circular that it can no longer tell which is which.

Foundations of Behaviorism

With these inquiries Pavlov launched behaviorism and behavioral psychology, a field that has grown immense over time, with notable contributions from Edwin Guthrie, John B. Watson, and B.F. Skinner, to name a few. It's a study that attracts criticism, both of its methods and conclusions. There is a reticence to believe

The Man in the Box

An autographed photo of Ivan Pavlov always hung behind the desk of at least one influential successor in the school of behaviorism, an iconoclastic psychologist diverted in his early twenties from writing poetry and fiction. He would eventually publish one notably successful novel, *Walden Two*, albeit a slow-motion bestseller, a utopian oddity that moved apathetically off the shelves for twenty years until its rediscovery in the countercultural 1960s. The author, B. F. Skinner, enjoys a kind of notoriety seldom accorded a scientist; mention of his work generally brings on a shudder—images of "Skinner boxes" full of pigeons, rats, and other animals programming themselves into behaviors willed by an unseen master scientist. And yes, one of his daughters indeed spent much of her infancy in a rather comfortably outfitted box, yet somehow grew fine and happily, despite persistent rumors to the contrary.

Ideas like Skinner's, that pigeons and ourselves learn and persist in doing things we are rewarded for, aren't necessarily the stuff of nightmares. But setting about manipulating behavior, and with the full weight of scientific method behind it, provokes uneasiness. What tremendous power for good or evil, one thinks, to turn out "well-behaved" units who needn't be let in on the plan. Away with Skinner!

Skinner's investigation of conditioning is often confused with advocacy, which is to mistake the messenger for the message. He certainly supported no ideal plan of behavior, but intended to describe the way behavior *is*. If reinforcement, or the lack of it, operates in consistent ways to shape what we know and do, then it's merely another fact, like the number of neutrons in a nucleus of uranium 235. Still, it seems a harsh reduction of human complexity and potential, from thoughtful judges of our surroundings to dimly aware entities careening through experiences we don't control. Have we deceived ourselves about knowing what we're doing? Were there any choices? It doesn't help assuage any sense of loss to find Skinner's views summed up in a volume entitled *Beyond Freedom and Dignity*—he liked ruffling feathers.

On the cheerier side of "operant conditioning" (experimental subjects "operate" on the environment, pushing levers and such, to find what actions produce rewards), nothing but *positive* reinforcement actually led to reliable results. What a behaviorist might observe, as Skinner did, in an average school classroom appalls the scientist: so little consistency, so much negative inducement (to perform, to get the homework done), no real accommodation for individuals all trying to find their own levers to make the environment work in a positive way. Out of this Skinner formulated the concept of programmed learning, with attainments that can be reached along individually evolved schedules and paths—teaching machines suggested themselves as a practical means; human teachers in sufficient numbers cost more and work less predictably.

Of course, the approach is only as good as its programs; the business of being the mastermind, the programmer, requires a kind of plasticity not generally found among dictators. Skinner once summarized the rules in his "four principles of scientific practice": when you run into something interesting, drop everything else and study it; some ways of doing research are easier than others; some people are lucky; and apparatuses, especially complicated ones, break down.

Albert Einstein [1879-1955]

Above: *Einstein came to symbolize the aspirations of the twentieth century, for a universe made knowable, for peace and tolerance in our small part of it. The public seldom understood his work but revered the archetypal absent-minded genius who made time crazily mutable.*

standards of genius, contributed deep understanding to the problems within the space of a single year.

The only autobiography of Einstein (written in 1948 for P.A. Schilpp's *Albert Einstein: Philosopher-Scientist*) drops few hints that the author ever lived anywhere outside of his capacious mind. His recollections are all of ideas and the directions in which they led his thinking. But we know, even if Einstein didn't consider it biographically consequential, that he lived robustly, if modestly, married twice, played the violin decently, wrote and corresponded on many non-scientific topics, and had a passion for world peace and Zionism. (He was offered the presidency of Israel in 1952, but declined.)

He was born in Ulm, Germany, to "entirely irreligious (Jewish) parents." Business travels eventually took the family to Italy and Switzerland, where Einstein's formal education was completed at the Polytechnic Institute of Zurich. After his initial publications, with an academic future assured, he lectured in Prague, Zurich, and then Berlin. The Kaiser Wilhelm Institute stood at the pinnacle of the physicist's world. Or rather, it occupied that position until 1933, when its distinguished Jewish professors were expelled and their possessions seized. Einstein accepted an invitation from Princeton's Institute for Advanced Study. And there he stayed, collaborating occasionally with the brightest minds of succeeding generations and continuing his own investigations (often in pursuit of a "unified field theory," which eluded him through the decades). He had the satisfaction, however, of seeing his relativity theory pass all the tests devised for it in the years since he'd first stood the scientific world on its ear.

By 1905 fundamental physics was unravelling. Max Planck's disagreeable discovery of energy emission and absorption at discrete levels hobbled classical theories. Albert Michelson and Edward Morley confirmed the scientific community's worst suspicions about light—not only was its speed a universal constant, no limping mechanical aids to rationalizing the fact, such as the ether, had any detectable basis in reality. Albert Einstein, in a virtuoso performance even by the

Understanding Relativity

The theory of relativity is in fact two theories: the special theory (concerning electromagnetic phenomena; published in 1905) and the general theory (about gravity; published in 1916). The problem of constant lightspeed belongs to the special theory—a logical starting place for examining the paradox in which Newtonian mechanics had become enmeshed.

Constant lightspeed means that all experimentalists, at rest or in motion relative to one another, will obtain the same result (186,282 miles per second, or 299,792 km/sec, in ideal vacuum conditions) when measuring the velocity of light. Now, if two observers—they always seem to be in spaceships, which we'll label Alice and Bert—are moving toward each other at some fancifully high velocity, say one-half c (c denotes the speed of light) and are overtaken by a light ray originating somewhere behind Alice, what do intuition and classical mechanics say each of them will find in measuring the velocity of this single light ray?

Never mind the addition and subtraction. The real answer is 186,282 mi/sec for both observers. Intuition and sturdy household physics argue, however, that Alice will clock the light ray at one velocity, while Bert must find a proportionately higher value. The light ray and Bert, after all, are rushing at each other with a large combined velocity which, it would seem, must be greater than the light ray's overtaking speed relative to Alice. There's nothing illogical or defective about such reasoning. Anyone who supposed the everyday world worked any differently would be a menace, even in light traffic, and might find life intolerably dangerous except in situations characterized by a physics of ideal simplicity, like bowling.

All Time Is Not The Same

All of this is well and good, except that it's completely wrong for light. Careful, repeated measurement confirms that light *does not* have a velocity that can be added and subtracted—like relative driving speeds—for observers with different velocities. Lightspeed *is* a constant. What effect does the constancy of c have on the way Alice and Bert perceive events unfolding? Alice, after ascertaining c on her equipment, should she look out to Bert, will allege that Bert's clock is running slower than hers and that his yardsticks are too short. By Alice's reasoning, if Bert comes up with c, it's only because he's doing science with dodgy instruments—she thinks he should have come up with a value somewhat higher. Bert, meanwhile, has formed precisely the same opinion of Alice's apparatus. Somehow the images conveyed by light between the spaceships are erroneous, systematically shortening lengths along the direction of travel and displaying a slower time.

Obviously, something—something classical—has to give. What explanations can be put forward? Might a photon act with perverse intelligence, speeding up or slow-

Below: The light ray would seem to be rushing at Bert with much greater speed than its overtaking pace for Alice, yet both observers will clock the ray at the same speed, c. Bert looks unnaturally gangly to Alice, too, because of her contracted view of things; Alice would appear similarly foreshortened to Bert.

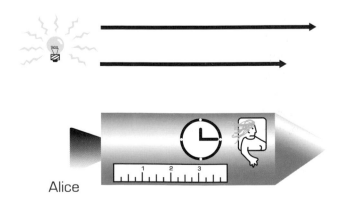

Alice

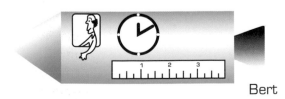

Bert

ing down just enough so that every observer will find the same value? Not an attractive theory. Might some agent act between spaceships to retard or advance light? Afraid not; that's the ether, and it was thrown out by Michelson and Morley. What about the measuring equipment, could it be gaffed somehow so as to register the value c whenever light runs through it? Also not an attractive theory, but much closer to the truth.

Certain logical conclusions follow from the apparent fact of constant lightspeed, namely, that if all observers regardless of motion must find the same value for c, then velocities among them cannot simply be added together—or else light really would have to speed up and slow down to overtake everyone at precisely c. Far more reasonable to assume that we've made some basic error about the way measurements are made. Most measurements, as in this case, come down to clocks and rulers, about whose construction we have no reason in principle to suspect infirmity. Better, as Einstein posited, to look for infirmity in time itself. Physicists and everyone else had long believed time passes at the same rate for all observers, everywhere, regardless of state of motion or any-

thing else. In the new understanding, since relativity, this is not the case.

Systems like spaceships, particles, or planets in motion relative to one another are often called *frames*—everything is considered its own "frame of reference," hence the shorthand usage of physicists. A frame experiences its own local time, called "proper" time, which goes at the same rate, so far as you may subjectively or mechanically judge, for any frame you happen to be part of. Frames in relative motion, however, will not find their proper times agree. Further, the difference in time rates is not arbitrary; times are related by an expression that makes everyone's numbers come out exactly right for insuring that all measurements of c reach the same result. Is this merely an illusion? Partly. Nothing really happened to the clocks and rulers as far as their owners can tell—but the effects implicit in the illusion are quite real. After years of travelling by different routes and accelerations, should Alice and Bert reunite, their quite good clocks will disagree as to how much time has elapsed since last they met; more time has gone by for one of them.

The Significance of Acceleration

So, if Alice and Bert seem to be having parallel and complementary hallucinations about their clocks, how is it that one of them may have aged more quickly than the other—this seems highly asymmetrical and unfair. The answer involves acceleration, more completely dealt with in the general theory. But briefly: while Alice and Bert are in relative, unaccelerated motion, there is no way to distinguish among them or, for that matter, a third observer who imagines himself at rest relative to both spaceships. Everyone's opinion about who is moving and who is not carries equal perceptual weight; that their clocks are running at different rates seems an exotic little fact of no palpable consequence. Acceleration is, however, a different case.

Below: Einstein watches a demonstration of transatlantic radio communication with a group of engineers, including (at his left) the great Charles Steinmetz and (at extreme right) David Sarnoff, later chairman of RCA. At this time, 1922, Einstein was only an occasional visitor to the United States.

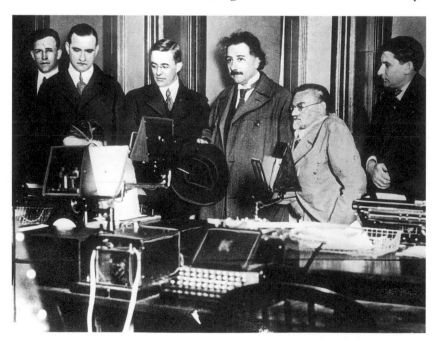

Left: Relativity, *an interpretation by the Dutch artist M.C. Escher. Linked through a bizarre, temporizing architecture, individual figures can retain only local notions of what is up, down, or sideways.*

Alice, for example, should she fire her rockets, would know from *g* forces or inertial resistance that she and not Bert was undergoing acceleration. Acceleration is not a kind of *relative* motion; it is absolute in that it's uniquely detectable and intrinsic to the frame in question.

Systems can arrive at disparate velocities or at mutual rest only through a series of accelerations. Acceleration slows time relative to unaccelerated or less accelerated frames. Acceleration, then, forces good clocks to part company in the time they keep. The greater the acceleration, the greater the difference in rates with which time passes. The longer one observer/frame spends at some steady, relative velocity after accelerating away from another frame, the larger the cumulative time difference between the two will grow—assuming they've arranged to accelerate to a future rendezvous at mutual rest and can actually compare clocks and calendars. Though real in every sense, actual elapsed time differences will be all but undetectable unless acceleration achieves relative velocities of a few tenths of lightspeed or better. Experiments with fast jets carrying ultra-accurate cesium clocks have confirmed the effect.

Why Lightspeed Must Be Constant

A true and verifiable rule for lumping frames and their motion-states together must modify Newtonian thinking in some way. Frame comparisons won't stand up without the conversion factor *c*, rather like a sliding handicap or a universal index for computing frame relationships. Lightspeed is not a conventional sort of velocity, like that associated with rolling stones or any kind of matter. Rather, it arises as a natural law out of what Einstein termed the relativity principle: There are no privileged observers in the universe; no place that is milepost zero, no state that is

Right: *Albert Michelson, in 1931, conducts light-speed measurements using a mile-long evacuated tube. The results fall within sixty millionths of a percent of today's accepted value. His most famous experiment, with Morley forty-four years earlier, looked for interference effects only and took up much less space—just a corner in the lab at Case School of Applied Science (now Case Western Reserve).*

absolute rest, no direction that is up or down. With no markers to settle questions about who is moving and who is not, we are obliged to discover a consistent way to relate all the comings and goings in the universe without playing favorites. We must, then, adopt the view that frames keep track in terms strictly of the one constant measure they hold in common, which is lightspeed. The implications are puzzling: if *c* cannot be fudged, then the very means of measuring *c* (clocks and rulers) must somehow compensate among observers. Time isn't anywhere in the universe available from a master chronometer and may go at a different rate for one frame as reckoned by another.

The Mathematical Explanation

In Einstein's thinking the problem turned on finding a way of reducing relative motions to some form that recognizes no special observers. Mathematically, this suggests abolishing special coordinate systems. Ever since Descartes, physical descriptions have usually been built up by plotting along the axes of a graph how a point moves through successive increments of time, distance, or whatever. Any frame may be thought of as its own coordinate system, charting the paths of other frames in reference to itself. The axes of coordinate systems are usually taken to be mutually perpendicular, though axes making arbitrary angles to one another could certainly be employed. Translating information from one skewed graph to another is accomplished by a simple formula called a transform. Something of the sort would seem to be needed in relativity theory, for the skewed perceptions Alice and Bert formed of each other's measuring apparatus is equivalent to saying they've found each other's coordinate systems to have started leaning. Moreover, the *time* ordinate is leaning, not just the conventional *x*, *y*, and *z* of familiar three-dimensional graphs. Time, *t*, loses its traditional independent status and must be thrown in with the others as a mutually dependent variable—a revolutionary state of affairs.

Finding the right transform is a problem in differential geometry, specifically of finding a way to express what remains unchanged, invariant, in drawing a line plotted on one graph onto another graph with a different slant to its coordinate axes. In this case, picture a square-ruled graph that has a tendency to compress itself by a scissor-like action in all its intersections. Certain ratios among the sides or angles of this flexibly jointed grid remain unaltered. Distances—paths from one point to another—can indeed be given in invariant form if properly expressed in an unstable grid's constant ratios. A distance derived in this way is usually called an *interval*; the specific rules of measurability constitute the *metric* of this geometry. With some trepidation, and at least a glance at one formula giving the relativistic interval for points in a unified *space-time*, we can apprehend the special theory much as Einstein presented it:

$$ds^2 = c^2dt^2 - (dx^2 + dy^2 + dz^2)$$

In this equation, *ds* is the interval. The squaring of all the terms may suggest something vaguely familiar, for it's nothing more than a four-dimensional version of the Pythagorean Theorem—the square of the hypotenuse is equal to the (alge-braic) sum of the squares of the other two sides of a right triangle.

This particular metric implies a *timelike* universe. Subtraction of the spatial parts (*x,y,z*) always leaves a balance in the interval's time component—which only confirms the hints and clues of observation. Two rocketing observers, arriving finally at mutual rest, find their clocks now running at the same rate, their rulers in perfect agreement, yet any time balance accrued between them in the course of travel remains. Our kind of universe, then, is characterized by timelike separations.

Why Lightspeed Cannot Be Exceeded

Were it a metric whose interval, *ds*, turned out always to be zero, implying no separation at all between events or points, the universe would be *lightlike*; that's a universe as "seen" by light, utterly lacking in elapsed time and strange indeed to contemplate. Should the interval become negative, less than zero, the result, as you might suppose, is a *spacelike* universe, in which everything is constrained to go faster than light and in which, should we

Below: Alice, once again, viewed in acceleration (rendered as a tilt) but employing the schematic conventions, light cones, of Minkowski's world geometry. Arrows tracking successive positions of a light cone define a "world line." Alice's right turn in space-time is apt to bring her into timelike contact with the police but take her clear of a historic first meeting with nonterrestrials— now just a spacelike possibility lost because it falls outside the directional limits of her cone.

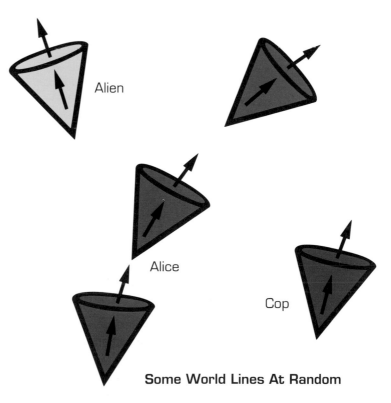

Alien

Alice

Cop

Some World Lines At Random

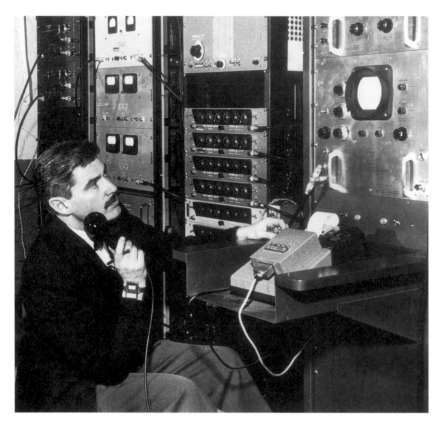

Above: In 1960 at Harvard, R.V. Pound concluding a delicate test of a gravitational red-shift predicted in the general theory. Some extremely fine lines in an iron isotope's absorption spectrum shifted in the expected way at slightly different elevations in Earth's gravitational field.

glimpse it (and we cannot), time appears to flow in reverse.

If you've followed the argument for timelike separations, you will suspect in this metric that spacelike separations must somehow accumulate. Would these be odd dislocations, normally inadmissible ways of getting from one place to another? Or, more exactly, is this the way things would appear from our timelike viewpoint? Guesses like these aren't really testable.

One of Einstein's former professors, Hermann Minkowski, created a useful way of representing the relativistic view. His "Minkowski diagrams" (we'll use cones) place an observer at any instant of time at the apex of a cone. The sides of the cone form a boundary, the *event horizon*, beyond which time separations would be too great for any event on the other side ever to be seen by the observer. A moment-to-moment succession of these cones—*light cones*—traces a moving *world line* for the observer. And taken all together, it adds up to a new connectability of things, *space-time*.

All that is potentially knowable to an observer, and is consequently within the cone's sides, belongs to the timelike universe; the sides themselves are lightlike; and outside the cone lies a spacelike wilderness (sometimes called "elsewhere"). Light cones make ready sense, but the "world geometry" worked out by Minkowski to go along with them led Einstein to remark: "Since the mathematicians have invaded the special theory of relativity, I do not understand it myself anymore."

Since the publication of Einstein's theories, everyone knows that you can't go faster than the speed of light. (Actually, anything that can make a difference, that carries information, that causes the minutest change, is restricted to lightspeed.) That should seem a less arbitrary dictum in view of the unique nature of *c*. What would it mean, after all, to travel at the speed of light? For one thing, you simply cannot make headway against *c*. Instead, as you continue to accelerate away from a given frame, say Earth, the wavelength of overtaking light stretches progressively until it is infinitely long. At this moment, it blinks out, a red shift to the vanishing point. Space-time communication fails; you have escaped Earth's light cone.

The Meaning Of $e = mc^2$

The famous equation $e = mc^2$ means, among other things, that any frame starting at rest relative to you will have to convert 100% of its mass to energy to reach lightspeed. In other words, it will become light. Anything attaining lightspeed attains light status, to be perceived and measured as energy. The shortening of yardsticks and slowing of clocks noted in Alice and Bert (*spatial contraction* and *time dilation*) dramatically increase as velocities approach *c*. Precisely as *c* is reached, spatial extension shrinks to zero and elapsed time stops, signalling entry into a lightlike state. What this means in concrete terms is hard to assess. We may only note that any frame clocked by Alice at less than *c* will register a speed less than *c* for *any* other voyager also travelling under the limit. Nothing actually edges out the door of the universe, no matter how sub-light velocities are concatenated.

If, by whatever trick of the theorist's imagination, objects do reach velocity greater than *c*, the result is that we won't ever have the chance to be aware of them. They lie beyond our event horizon. Not that physicists haven't tried: they've arranged indirect scenarios for detecting "tachyons," searching for time-reversed effects, but without success. Similarly, we cannot say what may lie beyond the edge of the visible universe because it's beyond lightspeed contact with us, beyond any meaningful discussion of "where," or "how fast."

Dealing With No Fixed References

Lightspeed, then, is the central element in a universal tautology, that which unifies spatio-temporal events in a consistent metric without recourse to absolute starting points or absolute velocities. As there is no other fixed reference in the universe, frames are scaled against each other. All the shrinking and slowing that goes on in relativity is an adjustment among frames that terminates eventually in their passing beyond knowledge of each other. If there were a gauge to register these changes, it would not be marked off zero to *c*, but rather in energy units expended in separating, accelerating one frame from another. Driven against its endstop, the gauge's needle records an extreme at which framelike relations cease to be possible.

But why should a cosmic operator like *c,* pure as thought itself, take on exactly the unsuggestive and actuarial value 186,282 mi/sec? If, as Einstein believed, God doesn't play dice, how did He throw a big 186,282 for lightspeed? The answer, of course, lies in the arbitrariness of our chosen units, whose origins are drowned

in cultural history extending back as far as Sumeria. As Einstein remarked, if *c* were represented in more *natural* units, as for instance the time light takes to travel 1 cm, the term *c* itself vanishes from the equations.

The General Theory Of Gravity

Moving on to relativistic investigation of gravity, the general theory, Einstein postulated conditions in which accelerated frames may be treated in a way similar to unaccelerated frames, *i.e.,* that a transform should relate them. Here, however, the problem is of considerable complexity. Coordinate systems belonging to accelerated frames are curvilinear, suitably imagined as grids drawn on rubbery surfaces that may be tugged, stretched, and deformed in any continuous way. Transforms among them are mathematical entities called *tensors.* The most consistent gravitational tensor implies spaces of positive curvature, like a sphere. (Special relativity is "flat" in the sense that it's a limiting, linear case of the simplest choice of tensor.)

The general theory finds gravity to impart shape to space; in other words, matter itself creates and molds the space in which it moves. The behavior of matter in a gravitational field only points up the contours of space in that region. Of course, gravity is an accelerating force, which means that interval calculations will show timelike separations for nonequivalent paths through a field. With increasing acceleration, a stronger field, time slows. At the center of a sufficiently massive body, with a consequently massive field, time stops altogether—but that brings us perilously close to black holes, treated elsewhere.

Einstein pointed out, as well, that objects always follow those contours in space that require the least expenditure of energy. Such paths are called *geodesics.* This can lead to some novelty in the way we think

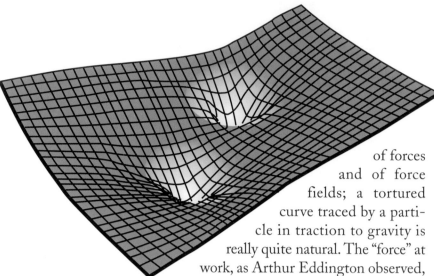

Above: A field representation, sometimes called an "embedding diagram," of Earth and moon in orbit. The gravity wells of each create in the space between them a shallower depression, which is the force of their mutual attraction. Matter shapes space.

of forces and of force fields; a tortured curve traced by a particle in traction to gravity is really quite natural. The "force" at work, as Arthur Eddington observed, is nothing more than the conceptual difference between the natural geometry of the place and our rather rectilinear expectations. If a straight line is the shortest distance between two points, then geodesics are nature's straight lines, for they are always the least-energy paths available between those points.

If anything is clear from relativity, it's the need to understand that frames possess a local time and a local space, all of which are distanced from other frames by relativistic intervals. That's what Einstein's equations are used for. Local time also implies that passing observers cannot certify that two distant (*i.e.*, spatially separated) events happen at the same time; there is no simultaneity of distant events. While some clocks may find two distant events concurrent, clocks of another locality, of another frame, are not bound to be timing things the same way. There are no privileged clocks.

Effect Before Cause?

Can the clocks be so far out of step one of them actually records a cause happening after its resultant effect? May broken eggs reassemble themselves, at least as seen from some carefully selected viewing frame? No, the theory doesn't fall into this kind of absurdity. Events close enough to each other to be causally con-

nected don't yield reversed intervals for any potential onlookers. Close-enough events have the property Einstein called *locality*. It must be mentioned, however, that some solutions of the gravitational equations, carried out by Kurt Gödel, permit a traveller moving in a wide circuit of the universe to return to his starting point at a time prior to his departure. What this means, physically, is anyone's guess; performing the experiment doesn't seem likely.

On the other hand, in everyday experience not so many frames are moving fast enough for any of this rather profound theory to make a difference. Old-fashioned Newtonian physics can cope. It's usually when looking toward the heavens that things break down. Galaxies do steam at relativistic velocities, gravitational crunches are occurring everywhere. It is well to know the truth even if you haven't much use for it.

Though relativity must take primacy of place in Einstein's work, his scientific achievements extend much further, into quantum mechanics and thermodynamics. While it is no secret he felt uneasy about the foundations and physical interpretation of quantum mechanics, he provided a quantum understanding of photoelectric effect and developed the Einstein-Bose statistics of particles with symmetric wave functions (*i.e.*, bosons, particles with integer spins, like the photon).

Together with Podolsky and Rosen he observed as early as 1935 that quantum theory cannot stand up without including something very like "action at a distance," something which might disturb the order of cause and effect—an idea that even today can precipitate allergies in physicists. In fact, it's become a leading topic for research and theory. Einstein's verdict? Action at a distance, *nonlocality*, "remains thinkable." One gathers that Einstein wouldn't wish to inhabit a universe in which it cannot be explained.

Stretching Physics

If you've had difficulty forcing your mind around some of the knobs and protuberances of modern physics, you will understand the feelings of the professionals—the physicists—upon whom relativity theory was foisted during the opening years of this century. Had not a few leading minds, Henri Poincaré foremost among them, digested and analyzed the theory in stunningly short order, relativity might have languished for a decade in conjectural limbo. That Poincaré—an expert on celestial physics—might venture where others paused is a mark of his brilliant mathematician's nature. To the mathematician Poincaré, a new world geometry of space-time possesses no more technical improbability than, say, Jacobi's six-dimensional phase space; to the physicist Poincaré, Einstein's elegant fields nicely fitted the special case that is the observable universe.

Poincaré had attended a conference in 1904 to discuss a widely felt sense that physics wasn't running well. The most obvious symptom was lightspeed. Michelson and Morley's delicate experiments in 1887, racing light in several directions around a mirrored track, had established an invariant velocity. Physics had patched up its resultant internal inconsistencies first with the Fitzgerald contraction, to make relative lengths come out right, and then with the combined Lorentz-Fitzgerald contraction to solve for an increase in mass. But scientists at the time realized they were in the position of schoolboys cribbing an answer on the algebra exam without being able to show their work. The answer, in fact, looks pretty ordinary (solving for time):

$$t_v = \frac{t_s}{\sqrt{1-(v^2/c^2)}}$$

where t_v is time passing for a clock moving at velocity v as perceived and measured by a stationary clock t_s; c is lightspeed. This is ordinary mathematics, but with disquieting effect for the real world. For example, should you and a twin adopt eerily circumscribed lifestyles, one travelling more or less nonstop at the legal speed limit for the next ten years, while the other puts up in a hotel room with limitless room service, the formula says (at 55 mph) the moving twin will have ticked off a millionth of a second less than the stationary twin at the ten-year mark. Should the twins repeat the experiment at illegal speeds, 580 million miles per hour or so, the time discrepancy grows apace, only five years going by for the traveller while ten has passed for the hotel guest. If v is allowed to approach c, the rate of time loss steepens dramatically.

Almost any absurdity seemed possible in the world the turn-of-the-century physicists had to cope with. The wonder is that the conundrums were disposed of so completely and quickly. One hastens to add that today's world still runs in disjointed time, but, thanks to Einstein and others, we can see the reasons now, how and why it must be so.

Below: The Michelson-Morley apparatus was mounted on a massive sandstone slab floating in a mercury pool. Once set in motion its slow spinning continued for hours. In actual practice several compensating refractions and longer paths (of multiple reflections) were employed—a tricky set of adjustments. At no angle relative to Earth, the rest of the universe, or the putative ether were differences detected in light-travel times along the two routes.

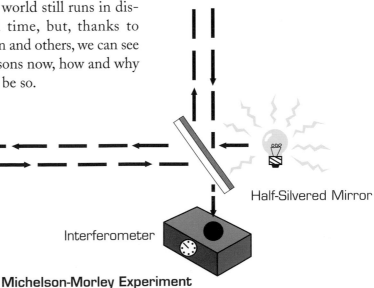

Half-Silvered Mirror

Interferometer

Michelson-Morley Experiment

Werner Heisenberg [1901-1976]

Before looking at Heisenberg's role in developing quantum theory, a few observations may be useful: First, familiar ways of explaining things in the large world of experience often don't work for quantum phenomena. Language seems to be deficient in terms to capture the wanted meanings. Second, perhaps no other theory has been more thoroughly tested or performed more impressively. Quantum theory doesn't have a single "discoverer"— many of the early nineteenth-century luminaries in physics had a hand in it. Among them were Max Planck, Albert Einstein, Louis de Broglie, Paul Dirac, Erwin Schrödinger, Arnold Sommerfeld, Niels Bohr, Max Born, Wolfgang Pauli, and—of course—Werner Heisenberg. Evolution of the strange new physics really got underway around 1913 with Bohr's model of the hydrogen atom, in which its electron could circulate around a nucleus only in certain allowed orbital paths. Schrödinger later showed that its orbital length was precisely a whole number of the electron's calculated wavelength.

Wavelength? Of a *particle* like the electron? Already experience begins to fail. Waves and particles had always seemed to be mutually exclusive categories. But Einstein's 1905 paper on photoelectric effect had backed up experimental hints that light, the most indubitably wavelike of all phenomena, also possesses a particle nature. A famous 1924 equation of de Broglie derived the converse, associating all particles with waves whose frequencies related to mass and velocity, or momentum. The mathematical pivot in this curious duality is Planck's constant.

Electrons Don't Behave Like Planets

As it turns out, the calculated wavelengths of everyday bits of matter are exceedingly short: undulatory teacups and such are definitely out of the picture, at least for any teacup appreciably larger than an electron. Only at that tiny scale do the conventional massy attributes of matter begin to fray. With this understanding, physicists could account for electron behavior in fine detail: an electron occupies only those orbital levels permitted by its frequency, which in turn is dependent on its energy. Should it jump to any permitted higher or lower level, it must absorb or radiate (as light) precisely the right amount of energy to "tune" its frequency to the next level.

Bohr's picture, together with the refinements of Schrödinger, settled a nagging problem left over from classical thinking, which had supposed that electrons behaved in the same purely material fashion as planets going round a star. But planets, sooner or later, spiral into their suns. Electrons do not expire in that way. Proper thinking about electrons, as *matter-waves*, implies a *ground state*: a last, lowest, minimum frequency obtainable through the momentum-wavelength relation. There simply aren't any available modes of existence below the ground state, which is also the last, closest orbit to the nucleus.

For mathematical convenience, Bohr, Sommerfeld, and others introduced the *quantum numbers*: n (principal), l (orbital), m (magnetic), and s (spin). Briefly, they count wave nodes for the relevant equations. They are simple, whole-number coefficients (except spin, which may also take half-integral values of $+\frac{1}{2}$ or $-\frac{1}{2}$ for the electron) that uniquely and completely describe any electron in orbit around a nucleus. From experimental data, Pauli suggested his *exclusion principle*: that no two electrons orbiting the same nucleus can possess an identical set of quantum numbers.

Heisenberg Advances Quantum Theory

Essentially, these were the features of quantum theory as Heisenberg found it in 1925, the year of his first great contribution to the field. He had scarcely graduated from prestigious Göttingen University when he published his system of matrix mechanics. A deep contemplation of his results led him to doubt that fundamental, microcosmic events take place in a completely measurable way. His is a physics that intrudes into the thoughts of philosophers, much as Galilean physics so discomfited the Church. Regrettably, the prime of his career coincided with war-time isolation for German scientists.

Unlike so many distinguished physicists (Einstein, Pauli, Szilard, and Bethe, among

others), Heisenberg remained in Germany throughout the Nazi era. He led a team charged with designing a German atomic bomb—and became the subject of a bizarre Allied kidnap plan. Debate still continues as to whether the team, and especially Heisenberg, deliberately pursued unpromising paths toward the objective.

Fortunately, the groundwork of quantum theory belonged to earlier decades when ideas were freely exchanged among a small international group that proofed and challenged each new step. The first unifying formulation belongs to Heisenberg. His analysis was couched in an especially abstruse mathematical form—the language of matrices. Even mathematicians would prefer lighter reading material. Imagine

Above: Niels Bohr discovered that Planck's quantum theory allows for atoms which behave as stably in theory as they do in fact. If, as Bohr saw, the new atom seemed somewhat irrational in classical terms, physicists could nevertheless set out experimental circumstances in which classical and quantum pictures agree—his "correspondence principle."

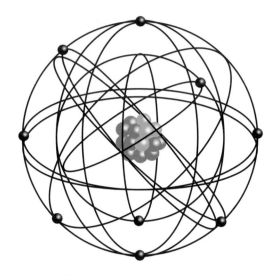

multi-dimensional surfaces turning within one another until certain sought after alignments and intersections are reached. On the printed page this amounts to vast number arrays which combine with one another by rules compounded in equal parts of grinding ennui and mad punctilio.

Had matrix mechanics remained the only way of displaying quantum theory, progress in physics might have slowed for a few years while scientists caught up with the mathematics. In 1926, however, Schrödinger presented essentially the same results in the more familiar form of wave mechanics. A proof offered by von Neumann demonstrated the equivalence of the two approaches, though its validity has been challenged by Dirac. Not that the information from either quantum perspective makes understanding it easy.

Both views cleared away an embarrassment arising out of de Broglie's otherwise successful equation. Calculated position for de Broglie's electrons occasionally ballooned to large volumes of space. Real electrons don't swell up. Schrödinger overcame this awkward inflation by deriving position and momentum as probabilities. Should one of de Broglie's electrons threaten to inflate, it signifies that the region in which that electron might be found has expanded, not the electron.

Probability Becomes
An Essential Ingredient

The implications of this finding are large. Should matter, so recently promoted to matter-wave status, now become a shadowy probability wave? Again, scale is decisive. Only when particle mass and wavelength are of comparable size does this theory cloud up. Teacups remain safe. Heisenberg saw where all this was leading—that measurements could not be made with arbitrarily fine precision. Locating an electron with great accuracy seemed always to destroy any chance of equal certitude in measuring its momen-

tum, and *vice versa*. This is not merely an experimental shortcoming, but an inescapable blurriness that is decreed in theory.

With the benefit of Heisenberg's insight, an initial guess can be made about the significance of probabilities in describing subatomic events. It cannot be assumed that a single particle follows a specific trajectory in travelling from one point to another. *All* permitted trajectories and states must be combined in proportion to their probabilities, a "sum over histories," to describe even a solitary particle's behavior. A path actually taken, if discoverable by experiment, only simplifies one part of the overall sum, and at the cost of enlarging the range of possible values for other particle properties. Two attributes, such as position and momentum, must swap probabilities back and forth.

Notice that what is being swapped is a degree of matter *vs.* wave identity. Neither aspect is more *real* than the other. It's a peculiar fact, but in quantum experiments the objects of interest always take on the appearance we've set out to find. Measures most pertinent to particle-like behavior invariably find particles and wave measures find waves. This is not the equipment's fault, nor any of the instruments'. Instead, there is an irreducible ambiguity about the nature of matter-waves. That ambiguity, thanks to quantum mechanics, can always be given a precise, formal expression. Stated quasi-mathematically: Multiplying two uncertainties together (as about position and momentum) equals some constant value because, as one decreases, the other must grow proportionately to yield a fixed result. And that eternally fixed result is Planck's constant, h, the quantum of action, that smallest increment of all allowed energy transitions.

The Uncertainty Principle Is Born

In a sense, asking for certainty greater than the equations allow is asking to see what lies in the undefinable gap between permitted energy states. Better apparatus cannot open up this dark place; a better theory might, if such were possible. For the present, Heisenberg's *uncertainty principle* seems certain. Any two values, like position and momentum or time and energy, that together would impose on a particle an un-Planck-like tidiness share the Heisenberg limitation. Such a pair of variables are often said to be "complementary"; their obligation to strike a balance of uncertainty is termed the *complementarity principle*.

In the quantum way of things, the words "absolute certainty" turn out to be no more meaningful than "bibbety-bobbety-boo." Expressing quantum sense with words like "particle" and "wave" hasn't worked well. And, as we shall see, having to speak of things like "collapse of the wave function" places an even greater burden on language. It is enough to know that the mathematics doesn't become tangled up in itself the way words and overly broad concepts do.

Where did this new theory leave physics? With a smeary electron, one whose "orbit" is a vague cloud darkened in the regions of higher probability. The wave component of this unspeakable electron entity can be split, like any other wave encountering a small obstacle, and made to rejoin itself in two out-of-step segments—it "interferes" with itself. Classical particles do not behave this way and waves

do not run into things the way electrons do. As a rule of thumb, when an electron has been "found" (detected as it bounces off something), it is a particle. At this moment, the wave part of its identity, associated with shifting probabilities, disappears—a physicist might say its wave function collapses.

Measurements and collapsed wave functions amount to the same thing: momentary states of certainty about position or momentum preceded and followed by states of unperfectable knowledge as to either. By way of contrast, imagine a prototype of a universe composed of billiard balls. Accurate position and momentum measurements of the scattered balls at any single instant would wholly determine the past and future of the system. We could mathematically run such a universe backwards and forwards like a movie.

Although such billiard-like, deterministic procedures do not apply to electrons, with enough of them an equally boring

Below: Otto Hahn (seated left), discoverer of atomic fission, physicist Otto Haxel (center), and Heisenberg (seated right) meeting with German government minister Josef Strauss. As members of the German Atom Commission, they are planning nuclear power production in a rapidly growing postwar Germany.

quantum movie could be made. A single electron, or photon, or any low mass-to-wavelength particle is free to act within its whole probable range. Large numbers of them, all constrained to act within the same range, begin to exhibit predictability. This is fundamental to the notion of probability: Expected patterns emerge through time or multiple trials. In ten thousand throws of a single die, two will come up about one sixth of the time. This is a bankable assertion. But the outcome of a single throw of an honest die is not similarly knowable.

The theory is beginning to sound a little trivial. Are hairs being split here about fleeting states of knowledge? A particle has only a probability of being here or there until it's actually found—which sounds as obvious as saying that the odds of finding an ace in the deck change as soon as you spot a pair of them hidden under the card table. The change in your information about aces and in your consequent estimate of the odds doesn't seem part of any thought-numbing mystery. But, parallels shouldn't be drawn too quickly. Quantum uncertainty embodies a deeper reality, as a few experimental findings will show.

Practical Applications of Quantum Theory

Recalling that a single particle-wave may interfere with itself, but only to the extent that it marks out a region of probability for its particle manifestation, how must photons from distant stars carry that property? The interference region, naturally, would spread a bit with distance, as any wave does as it travels. For stars at suitable distances from earth, the spread is a few tens of feet to many miles, easy enough to detect and mark its boundaries. Analysis of light from chosen stars has indeed confirmed the effect. The idea works nicely in reverse to measure stellar distances from earth by first finding the limits of an interference signal and calculating the distance it must have come to spread by that amount. This is information that conventional properties of starlight cannot provide.

In a related vein, quantum mechanics predicts that particles may show up in places where they shouldn't just because there is a (calculable) probability, however small, that they will. Electrons too weak to overcome a repulsive force may nonetheless "tunnel" through it. A num-

Right: In 1911, Ernest Rutherford, pictured here with H.W. Geiger, proposed the most familiar model of the atom: electrons orbiting at various distances a compact positive nucleus. Any hope of reconciling this Newtonian construct with observed atomic behavior had evaporated by 1913.

ber of electronic solid-state devices operate on this principle.

Twins and Hypercubes

Experiments along different lines—concerned with phenomena first conjectured by Einstein, Podolsky and Rosen, later investigated by Bell—appear to show that twin photons somehow "sense" the collapse of each other's wave function. "Twins" for such experiments are created in special ways so that certain properties, like polarization or total energy, always have known combined values. The results argue unequivocally for such photons existing in no predetermined state, collapsing variably to some measurable condition depending only on the state of a faraway twin, even though that twin's state may be altered somewhat before any measurement is made.

In quantum argot, a particle's states are *superposed*: neither one nor another, or all at the same time. Such a truly indeterminate condition is implicit in theory, but hard to demonstrate and even harder to believe. Worse still, these experiments seem to confirm a kind of action at a distance, an effect shared instantaneously, faster than lightspeed, between separated photons.

What can be made of this? With the repeated caution that quantum mechanics doesn't easily fit into language or pictures, consider the hypercube—a mathematical extension of an ordinary cube into four spatial dimensions. It's impossible to see it exactly in the mind's eye and it certainly can't be built. Some physical sense of it could be acquired, however, by constructing a series of three-dimensional (3-D) sections through it—analogous to passing a 2-D plane through a cone or a cube, and then examining the succession of 2-D views to which the 3-D objects have been reduced. A hypothetical 2-D being, then, could only build up knowledge of a 3-D world through analysis of 2-D sections.

Any quantum wave function only leads to real-world probabilities by squaring the expression (which gets rid of some troublesome square roots of negative numbers). The transition from quantum actuality (the world as it is) to measurable reality (the world we can make sense of) works only so long as we craftily dispose of imaginary numbers (like i) along the way. But they're still there, in the wave function, at some deeper level of structure.

The imaginary numbers make up the points along a fourth coordinate axis, "at right angles," as the mathematicians say, "to the other three." A few moments of trying to move four lines, rods, rulers, or whatever into a mutually perpendicular relationship will disclose that we are one dimension shy. This trick can't be managed with three dimensions, and no one is going to lend you another.

The Fourth Dimension

In light of this discovery, it might be supposed that quantum probability is a four-dimensional thingamabob. It might further be supposed that measurement of quantum phenomena is awfully close to cutting a 3-D piece out of the larger pie. Maybe a photon really does exist in superposed states; we'll never be able to see it (them?) that way because we've been dimensionally shortchanged. Or, maybe action at a distance is but an oblique way of observing something which is quite natural and unremarkable about how things connect up in extradimensional fashion. Our view is necessarily restricted to those "flattened" pieces of the truth that are representable to us. We can, then, only follow our mathematical inferences as to the nature of a hypercube, though with study we may pick up an intuitive feel for its unseeable shape.

One of the things quantum mechanics does better than any previous theory is to make predictions. Dirac noticed in 1930 that certain possible energy levels of electrons in his equations had not shown up in experiment. His mathematics seemed to call for negative energy states, which he chose to interpret as a condition of opposite electrical charge. It was clear that electrons in such a condition would annihilate the more familiar kind of electron, with both particles perishing in a flash of light. Allowable or no, the casual enormity of postulating an entirely new kind of matter—namely anti-matter—seemed an unlikely reach for a few mere calculations. Carl D. Anderson's discovery in 1932 of the positron (positive electron) dramatically boosted confidence in the anti-matter theory.

Predicting and finding particles became quite routine through ensuing years. Particle bookkeeping eventually recognized most of the new discoveries as mere transitional existences to stabler states within families of particles. Some particles—the *bosons*, such as photons and pions—carry the interactions between all the rest—the *fermions*, including electrons, protons, and neutrons. (The category names derive from separate probability behaviors for each. Pauli's exclusion principle applies only to fermions.) All of the electromagnetic phenomena have been wrapped up, chiefly by Richard Feynman, in quantum electrodynamics (QED). Subsequent work by Weinberg, Glashow, and Salam unified the weak nuclear force with QED into "electroweak" theory. Further probing into particle interiors turned up yet more particles—quarks, gluons—and added a new range of understanding, quantum chromodynamics (QCD). Taken together, electroweak theory and QCD make up a staggering maze rather disarmingly named the "Standard Model."

Even a Vacuum Has Energy
Even the void has been quantized. Theory finds that the vacuum itself must have energy and feel a certain pressure of probability. Particle/anti-particle pairs are con-

stantly bubbled into existence out of nothing. They perish so quickly, in a femtoblink of none-too-steady quantum time, that they are called "virtual particles." Where do they come from? Perhaps out of the Planck soup, that world of infinitesimals below the threshold h. Events at this level tax even quantum imagination. Time runs chaotically here—and so do physicists, who've posited as many as twenty-six dimensions, most of them looped closed at Planck scale and permanently lost to view.

With a theory in hand that is already burdensomely rich in results, unrestricted in breadth, and tolerably magical, what more can a physicist ask? The list isn't short. For one thing, relativity and quantum mechanics haven't been combined into any coherent universal scheme. They remain useful to each other and yet isolated in their separate domains. Gravity hasn't been a quantum success, either. Of the many models proposed to quantize gravity, none have survived close scrutiny. Three of the four fundamental forces (electromagnetism, strong and weak nuclear forces) have been united in quantum theory, each associated with its own particle, or quantum of interaction. The graviton, gravitational quantum, is only a name for the ghost which inhabits this part of the cosmic house.

Even more basic questions concern an unsettling reticence of current theory: Its equations cannot be made to spill out the glittering essentials, such as Planck's constant. A really good theory, the kind that would make physicists close up for lunch one day and never come back, should be able to derive its fundamental verities in an absolute way, without recourse to experiment and the limits of experimental error. Meanwhile, two sorts of anxiety afflict interested bystanders to the universe: that no Theory of Everything (TOE) will emerge, or worse, the ultimate understanding will be couched in a mathematics more inscrutable even than Heisenberg's.

One Very Small Number

At the very foundation of quantum mechanics lies a puzzling but rather innocuous observation about heated bodies made by Max Planck in 1899. It's another one of those cases where a small rough patch in a perfectly fine understanding of the world, namely the entire edifice of classical physics, is found to overlay a fatal crack in the basic structure.

It had always been assumed that energy radiation, most notably as visible light, must be available in a continuous spectrum. All wavelengths should show up in the output of some ideal radiating source, termed a "black body." In other words, a perfect black body should emit (or absorb) light in an unbroken progression of frequencies, like the smooth increase in a stereo's volume as its volume knob is turned. Ideal equipment is seldom available in laboratories, but serviceable approximations are. In 1895, Wilhelm Wien, utilizing an ingeniously-contrived heated sphere and tiny escape slit, carried out emission measurements that fell into a pattern of irregular peaks as energy delivered to his furnace grew or fell.

Wien's results left a general impression that theory would have to be refined. Some assumptions, particularly about short-wavelength light, would need cleaning up. Investigating the problem, Planck discovered he would have to abandon the notion of continuity, substituting for it a finely divided range of possible energy levels, as given by one of the most famous formulas in physics:

$$e = hv$$

where e is energy, v is frequency, and h is the constant, *Planck's constant*, that separates one energy level from the next.

Planck realized, further, that his equation implies that light is emitted in discrete quan-

tities, *quanta*, like particles or atoms of energy. That physics might have overlooked this possibility wasn't so surprising, in that h has the almost-vanishing value of 0.00000000000000000000000000066256 erg-seconds. (Erg-seconds are units of energy through time, called *action* in physics, and it's much easier to write the number as 6.62×10^{-27}.)

Planck's interesting results didn't imme-diately attract attention. The ultimate util-ity and truth of the quantum view emerged slowly. In 1905, Einstein incor-porated it into his description of the pho-toelectric effect. Niels Bohr developed a quantized model of electron orbits in the hydrogen atom in 1913, which finally answered such common-sense questions as to why electrons don't lose energy con-tinuously and spiral into the nuclei they orbit. Consequently, physicists would have to examine new paradoxes concerning the intertwined discrete and continuous prop-erties of matter and energy, simultaneous particle-like and wavelike behavior. The strongest formulation of quantum under-standing, the *uncertainty principle*, wasn't worked out until 1927—and its meaning is still being debated.

John von Neumann [1903-1957]

Above: *Von Neumann's brilliance encompassed both the mathematical and the practical.*

Opposite: *Another computer pioneer, T. Kite Sharpless (above), working with the 1952 vintage EDVAC. Three decades later, vastly more powerful computers had become child's play.*

Uncommonly bright minds are abundant in the fields of mathematics and physics, but only a rare few, like Gauss or Poincaré, seem to draw from an inexhaustible fund of insight. John von Neumann belongs to that dazzling group. Revered by his colleagues for his quickness and encyclopedic breadth, von Neumann left scarcely any branch of mathematics and physics untouched. He appeared at critical points in widely diverse parts of the twentieth-century mathematical world with a frequency that was almost uncanny.

When Gödel first read his soon-to-be-a-blockbuster theorem to a gathering of mathematicians in 1930, no one seemed to get the point, which was that the whole of the subject had just been put on a new footing, with unpredictably limited deductive power. Von Neumann absorbed it and rushed into a private discussion with the young Viennese logician. He immediately set himself to working out further implications for the foundations of logic.

As quantum theory was emerging in the 1920s, von Neumann constructed its axiom system, illuminating the theoretical futility of searching for ways to reconcile its puzzling uncertainty relations with traditional ideas of causality. And when a little-known English mathematician, Turing, published a strange paper on hypothetical machines and the boundaries of computability, von Neumann initiated an immediate correspondence. Between them, in 1937 they comprised pretty much the world's entire capacity for advanced computer design. The logical organization, the *architecture*, of most computers is still that of von Neumann, particularly in that problems are solved in sequential order—which distinguishes them as "von Neumann machines" in the theoretical argot.

A Mathematical Prodigy

That von Neumann was brilliant, perhaps a good deal more than brilliant, had been clear even in childhood. Born in Budapest to an affluent banking family, he received a private education until his enrollment in a secondary school (gymnasium) at age ten. Within a short time, his teachers undertook to have him tutored in mathematics by university professors. Von Neumann had become a publishing, working mathematician by the age of nineteen. Much of his work at this time belongs to the realm of set theory, to which he contributed a generally preferred way of defining real numbers. In 1933, he was asked to join the newly created Institute for Advanced Study at Princeton University—his academic address for the rest of his life.

His amazing scope in both pure and applied mathematics put him in demand for several scientific projects during World War II, culminating in his participation in the Manhattan Project at Los Alamos to construct the first atomic bomb. In postwar years computers became a focus of his work. He developed ideas on the nascent technology—programming, error theory, reliability—both at mathematical and practical levels, and sometimes even visionary, such as considering the systems requirements for self-reproducing machines. And still he contributed in other fields, most notably a proof in 1955, just before his health failed, of the equivalence between the two leading expressions of quantum theory: matrix mechanics and wave mechanics.

Games and Strategies

Von Neumann's chief mathematical researches have a lot to do with Hilbert spaces, hermitian operators, and the paths from one algebra into the next, which is to say, the sort of thing that keeps graduate schools, and physics, in business. Something of a multidimensional operator himself, he appeared out of nowhere in 1926 with a completely unexpected piece of analysis inaugurating a theory of games—games like bridge, chess, and poker. Mathematics had already addressed some relevant issues: precise formulations of a player's probabilistic expectations had been around for a few centuries. But going any further, into complete *strategies* for winning, had always seemed to be bound up in imponderables: an opponent's unpredictability, level of intelligence, willingness to deceive, and so forth. Von Neumann wasn't deterred; as he discovered, behavioral variables needn't spoil the

usefulness of strategies. In fact, straying from what is mathematically best can only penalize a rash human player.

To begin, von Neumann classified games as either *zero-sum* or *nonzero-sum*. When one player's gains can only be made up from another player's losses, they are competing for larger or smaller slices of the same pie—a zero-sum situation. On the other hand, if in playing the game everyone's stake is somehow made to grow, it's conceivable all the players could finish ahead of the game—a nonzero-sum result. Most of what we ordinarily think of as games fall into the zero-sum category. Von Neumann, however, likened such things as economic activity to games: in the course of typical economic processes—investment, manufacturing, recycling—values to the players may grow, be recirculated, or change form. Here, in the nonzero-sum case, the pool of potential winnings isn't restricted to the stakes players brought with them.

Further defining his notion of games, von Neumann identified a *strategy* as that course of action, a series of plays, which guarantees minimum losses. His method, naturally, requires a way of setting out the result of every decision, tabulating for each possible "move" the effect of all possible countermoves by an opponent. This introduces some complexity into the theory, for cases must distinguish the number of players (two-person, three-person, *n*-person games), whether some moves are random, whether players move in sequence, with knowledge of previous play, or must make their decisions in the dark. The details took some time to tidy up, but he'd fit them all in by 1943 when he published, in collaboration with Oskar Morgenstern, *Theory of Games and Economic Behavior*.

The Minimax Theorem

This is good, clear-headed thinking but apt to lead to a dull, fine-print telephone book of strategies without some power-

ful generalization of the way strategies are arrived at. Drawing on the mathematics of matrices, von Neumann constructed the needed tool, his famous minimax theorem for solution of games. Examining the outcomes of play at any stage, it's always possible to point out at least one value that is the best of the possible bad results, and at least one that is the least of all good outcomes. (They're usually known as the "maxmin" and the "minmax," which makes them sound somehow motorized.) *If* it happens that the maxmin and the minmax coincide, it would give a perceptive player the opportunity to find a move that always insures a minimum of loss—which minimum can certainly turn out to be a positive amount; a player would have to be perversely motivated to continue in a game known by the minimax theorem to result in inescapable losses. Quite possibly, too, an informed player may fare better than his bare strategic expectation: should his opponent, perhaps a little less advanced in absorbing von Neumann, not reply with the best possible moves from his own minimax solution, then the winnings of a strategically correct player can only increase. The minimax is always the very *least* a good player can expect against an optimized counterstrategy.

Finding a simultaneous concurrence in this, the *value* of play, amounts really to deciding whether particular matrices *commute*, whether *xy* is the same as *yx*, and there's every possibility they won't. Von Neumann proved for all games in which the range of moves is known (*i.e.*, games with full information) that a coincidence of the two, a *saddle point*, must exist. Knowing only this, it can be asserted, for example, that chess is a foregone conclusion. Undoubtedly there exists a best possible strategy, for which the game cannot fail to end in the same outcome every time. Now, whether that unbeatable strategy gives white the win, or black, or neither

(stalemate) can't be calculated at present; the number of possible moves is enormous. Of course, chess was designed that way to make it interesting to humans. Computers, which handle enormous numbers differently than mere humans, might solve the game someday, tossing it into the heap of things not worth doing anymore.

It's even possible, where some element of chance enters in, to find a best possible mix of strategies, to plan the percentages with which certain moves should be employed within an overall strategy. (Von Neumann illustrated the case with an amusing contest of the minds between Sherlock Holmes and Dr. Moriarty, each attempting to anticipate the moves of the other in a train pursuit.) Gratifyingly, the theory generates rich strategies even under simplified assumptions, prescribing that poker players should bluff if they wish to win, or realistically simulating the determination of price in a market. But the theory has its limits. One of them, illustrated in the example of chess, is the staggering size of some computations needed to materialize an actual strategy. Such situations arise fairly often in mathematics. Neither can the theory prescribe a strategy where none exists: in a game of pure chance with identical odds on all outcomes—like flipping coins—game theory can't improve anyone's expectations by some mathematical sleight of hand. A pity.

In the sense that it's sometimes said Leibniz was the last man to know everything, von Neumann may have been the last to have a crack at everything. The basic stock of mathematics, science, philosophy, literature, music—all the things that somehow culturally "mattered" in Leibniz's day—didn't amount to so much more than a first-class genius could absorb in seventeenth-century Europe. No one else, human anyway, will ever have quite the same opportunity as Leibniz, though a few versatile minds—Poincaré has already been mentioned—were still able to comprehend an impressive portion of all mathematics and physics right into the twentieth century. This lineage, however, must come to an end with von Neumann. Pure mathematics and the knowledge of its applications are today an immense edifice of specialty, sub-specialty, cross-specialty all redoubling in volume by some invisible logarithmic law which doesn't yet have a name. Von Neumann, who moved as fast as anyone, took the last trip around the whole proverbial block.

Catastrophes and Reality

Right: *"Virtual reality,"*
illusions that shift three-
dimensionally to keep up
interactive contact with
an observer. Computers
routinely "build," operate,
and test objects whose
physical construction may
never take place.

Below: *Claude Shannon*
gave quantitative form
to information, general-
izing the nature of mes-
sages and noise from
concepts arising classi-
cally in thermodynamics.

Von Neumann's complete success in separating from the vagaries of human behavior a mathematical structure for all gamelike pursuits opened a floodgate in applied mathematics. The twentieth century has become as eager to subtly quantify complex behaviors as was the seventeenth century to organize the mechanical world into great laws of motion. In truth, such efforts were presaged by D'Arcy Thompson's *On Growth and Form* (1917), a unique bio-topological examination of the ways in which living forms may grow and transform themselves. Thompson's work shares with von Neumann's a dazzling method and a near complete lack of ancestry.

That pure cogitation might somehow impinge on affairs of the world had always been a cherished presumption of philosophers; in Galileo's day the church felt it had been blindsided when tinkerers with mere numbers began to decompose doctrine. Such a feeling of unexpected impact is a familiar one in the twentieth century. Putting the "laws" of thought (Boole's) and a lot of electronics into a computer, we spend a lot of time modelling the world—it's all numerical in form, yet we trust its "reality" because we've grown accustomed to the deep congruence of mathematical forms and the world of experience. Leaving aside for a moment the computer's undoubted knack for engineering, designing or testing airplane wings, drugs, and golf balls without so much as an atom of titanium to work with, if a computer says the sum of Wall Street wisdom amounts to an advantageless "random walk," or that "renormalizing" an opinion sample can predict voting behavior, then clearly this is mathematics *deluxe*.

In fact, practical computers probably couldn't work at all but for the fact that all information has properties quite similar to the thermodynamical demon called *entropy*. This was pointed out in 1948 by the originator of information theory, Claude Shannon. Besides its obvious importance in defining the very stuff that computers handle, this branch of applied mathematics is broad enough to make characterizations about music, language, quantum physics, and the genetic code—not only quantifying information content but suggesting how meaning itself arises. Approaching entropy from a different direction, what is known as chaos theory, leads to equally broad applications, often uncovering limits in the precision of conventional mechanistic methods—or why we'll probably never be able to make a really good weather forecast.

One more example, from a continuation of Thompson's thinking, is the abstruse

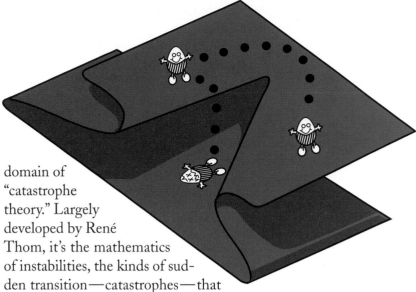

domain of "catastrophe theory." Largely developed by René Thom, it's the mathematics of instabilities, the kinds of sudden transition—catastrophes—that lie hidden in seemingly smooth processes. The method is topological: the behavior of mathematical functions or models is itself modelled upon generalized surfaces, only seven of them, which comprise the full structural nature of discontinuous change. The shapes of catastrophe, unfortunately, are for the most part *hypersurfaces*, only partially representable in three dimensions, though the simplest, "folds" and "cusps," fall within ordinary viewing range. By holding a dimension or two constant, decent pictures of "swallowtails" and "butterflies" can be drawn up. The remaining three, all "umbilics," are knottier spatial challenges.

In these catastrophes, a functional value, wandering through its range, suddenly drops off an infolding edge or a ridge, making for an abrupt landing—a sudden event. The analysis has proved useful in studying such things as chemical reactions, optics, elasticity, hysteresis, and even the extinction of species. Because of its generality the idea has been applied, with varying degrees of specificity and imagination, to growth, genetics, language, markets, revolutions, mental illness, and even art. There must be a point, as well—perhaps locatable on an umbilic—where the use of mathematics transforms into metaphor, though the rules aren't clearly understood.

Above: In a surface that plots the values of a function, it is a sudden transition, a quick remove to some other region, that makes a catastrophe. Smooth paths, avoiding precipitous change, are also possible, as on the swallowtail surface depicted here.

Alan Turing [1912-1954]

A curious, but reliable, fact about scientific papers is that they rarely bear titles that might attract attention or betray any hint of usefulness. "On Computable Numbers, with an Application to the *Entscheidungsproblem*," when it appeared in 1937, set perhaps a score of people in the world abuzz. But the article, beyond disposing of a large mathematical problem, introduced the hypothetical Turing Machine—a fertile and deep generalization about the way all problems are solved. The author of the article was Alan Turing, a strange but surpassingly creative mathematician.

Turing always possessed a childlike straightforwardness that tended to unsettle people. No doubt the shy Turing often came away unsettled, as well. His manner and youthful appearance often got him stopped by proctors enforcing the after-dark student curfew at Cambridge, where Turing lectured after 1935. He had, too, a fascination for what he called his "desert island game": using discards, leftovers, or simple raw materials to formulate household necessities such as utensils and tools. The object was to simplify his requirements. Turing fits the image of the distracted, slightly "off" sort of genius—it was no surprise when he was recruited at the beginning of World War II to work on breaking German codes.

At Bletchley Park, the wartime center for cryptanalysis, he created techniques to speed up decryption of messages produced by various models of the German Enigma machine. Though a working Enigma had been smuggled out through Poland just before that country's collapse—and, in any case, its principles were well understood—the code machine still presented difficulties to the Allied intelligence services. Inasmuch as its multiple rotor settings might be altered frequently (toward the end of the war as often as twice a day), deciphering messages had little practical value if the solutions weren't forthcoming for days. And, since many messages had no intrinsic value anyway, a great many had to be analyzed to disclose significant information. While Turing contributed to the mathematical methods used to solve codes, he and others realized more speed and crunching power were sorely needed.

The First Computer

Applying his genius to the problem, Turing designed an electronic monster, called Colossus, using the *Universal Turing Machine* described in his 1937 paper. The size of three large wardrobes, with 2,400 tubes, it processed thousands of characters per second. By contemporary standards, this beast wasn't as bright even as the automatic tuning circuit in an FM radio. But every technology has to start somewhere and Colossus was one of the first electronic computers—proof that his 1937 theoretical blueprint was valid.

Turing went to work for Britain's National Physical Laboratory immediately after the war, with ambitious plans for a larger, more versatile machine to be called ACE, the Automatic Computing Engine. A remarkably short-sighted government delayed and wavered over the project, so that Turing shifted his researches to the University of Manchester, which had a working computer, albeit a rather modest machine. His life ended tragically from a suicidal dose of potassium cyanide, which he probably prepared in one of his self-sufficient "desert island" projects.

During his tenure at Manchester, Turing had worked far ahead of accomplished technology, anticipating the shape of things to come. He began to model human intelligence with programmable machines and, in 1950, devised his famous "Turing test."

The Dawn of Artificial Intelligence

How can we satisfy ourselves that a machine is acting like a human? Can we know if it is conscious? (How, indeed, do we intuit that our own acquaintances are conscious?) Turing took a sideways tack, avoiding a long discussion of human awareness. It would be enough, he suggested, if a human being could be fooled by a machine. His experiment called for a human interrogator to teletype questions to unseen occupants of two rooms: one human and the other an advanced computer. Answers to the questions—any type of question—were to be evaluated to determine which respondent was human

and which electronic. If the questioner concluded wrongly, preferring the computer's collegial masquerade to the human, the machine would pass the test.

Turing had realistic expectations that such experiments would occur. Within fifty years of his writing, he predicted, machines with perhaps a gigabyte of memory should be able to outfox an average human interrogator 70 percent of the time in a five-minute session. In truth, computer programs were briefly engaging unwary humans in conversation within twenty-five

Above: "Colossus," Turing's giant with very little brain—but a starting place for the computer age.

Below: A somewhat smarter 1949 prototype at the University of Manchester. Bulk and waste heat were only reduced with the advent of transistors and, later, of micro-circuitry.

Above: A Turing Machine: in principle, it doesn't really matter how a device is induced to change state—right-left, positive-negative, even a few thousand people throwing light-switches on prearranged cues—all such machines process information in a similar manner.

years. A later, more sophisticated program, designed to pose as a psychiatrist, consistently escaped detection. (When informed of the deceit, some clients still preferred the computer.) And computers can be terrific at feigning *impaired* mental states: A program imbued with paranoid responses could not be distinguished from genuine patients by psychiatrists, whether or not they had been informed that a simulation was among the group.

All very well, but isn't this cheating? Maybe—the Turing test has loosened an avalanche of words. It seems a bit facile, too quickly disposing of the mystery we rather proudly hold to be bound up in human consciousness. We don't know, at present, whether *perfectly* satisfying the Turing conditions might also fill some deeper, ultimate specifications about which we humans could feel happier. A whole new field, the study of artificial intelligence (AI), has grown up around the problems of defining and duplicating consciousness. Neurophysiology, physics, and mathematics unite in efforts to understand and reproduce the human brain's operation.

Certainly it's as grand a project as science has ever embarked upon.

AI scientists, in print, are given to occasional gloom. In four decades of work what has been achieved, after all? Machines can play chess brilliantly and yet still stagger through simple mazes with less grace than a two-year-old and pick up language not as well as the toddler. The difficulty, and the success, has been in devising programs that instruct themselves—"learn"—from previous trials. Computers—once strictly "yes/no" processors—have been taught to rely on fuzzier estimates like "maybe" or "probably" to acquire rudimentary input and to test their own inferences.

Hardware on both sides—the aspiring machine, and the already evolved human—is fairly impressive. The human has one hundred billion multiply interconnected brain cells carrying electrical impulses at speeds up to 100 meters per second. A large computer is only an order of magnitude or so behind in number of "cells" (transistors) and processes electrical signals a million times faster. But a computer is put together linearly; information moves through it in a long train, one operation at a time. Brains appear to do many things at once. Parallel computing—for machines—is used increasingly, but entails enormous complexity in programming. Experimenters have designed circuits, smallish ones, with a more brainlike look, "neural networks," but there's no off-the-shelf theory for instructing one. Should it make a difference whether the machine is hooked together linearly or in network fashion? Here we return to the Turing machine and the *Entscheidungsproblem* with which Alan Turing opened the computer age.

The Tenth Problem

David Hilbert, the great German mathematician, proposed at the beginning of this century a list of twenty-three problems he believed most urgently needed to be solved, all part of "Hilbert's program" to put a solidly logical foundation under all of mathematics. Number ten, the *Entscheidungsproblem* ("decision problem"), called for a step-by-step procedure, an *algorithm*, for deducing all the propositions that are true within any mathematical system. Sounds a little like going through Euclid and proving each theorem in turn with the axioms and previous theorems, except that at the end, there's nothing to tell whether you might have missed proving something along the way. Hilbert wanted a foolproof method, if such exists.

In 1931, Kurt Gödel, an Austrian logician, demonstrated in a brilliant proof that any part of mathematics at least as complex as arithmetic (not so very complex, usually) can never be called complete. No algorithm, howsoever large, can lead to sorting out all the true or untrue expressions within the system. Moreover, Gödel's proof doesn't merely run things out to infinity and throw up its hands. He showed, using the structure of arithmetic, that expressions exist that cannot be reached by the rules of arithmetic proof. The expressions are *undecidable*—true, false, or somehow neither, arithmetic can have nothing to say about them. Hilbert's program had been torpedoed.

Consideration of the tenth problem by no means came to an end. Gödel's stunning result stimulated a broad interest in the nature of algorithms. Challenged, Turing followed a train of thought through the problem examining the basis of computability. He reasoned that if even the best deductive systems are doomed, it should be possible to think up a universal computing procedure and test it for expected failure. Imagine that a trouble-free proposition is fed into the truth-testing algorithm. Eventually, the proposition is definitively accepted as true or rejected as false and, if it were a machine, the algorithm could stop churning at this point, its work done. Given an undecidable case, however, no stopping place would ever be

reached. Turing called this the "halting problem": are there problems for which no algorithm will halt? This is an equivalent restatement of the *Entscheidungsproblem*.

Turing's Universal Machine
Turing began by picturing a basic machine, any mechanism capable of acting in a definite number of ways (even two ways are enough) as instructions are delivered to it one at a time. It doesn't matter whether this machine is conceived to fill some interesting purpose, merely that it carries out the procedures predictably as

Above: HAL, a co-star of 2001—A Space Odyssey: *humans and machine vying for the upper hand. Turing wondered how far consciousness might develop in computers.*

Below: The first major digital computer, ENIAC (Electronic Numerical Integrator and Calculator), built in 1942 to solve ballistics problems.

Above: *Turing (standing) and engineers confer at the console of the Ferranti Mark I (1951) at the University of Manchester. The British government was quick off the mark in supporting computer development but allowed such promising starts to languish after the war.*

instructed. Such a machine—the *Turing Machine*—may be thought of as a clockwork curiosity advancing a punched instruction tape through itself, perhaps raising and lowering a signal arm in response to its instructions. Or it may exist equally well on paper as a progression of symbols (numbers, letters, sketches, whatever) showing the state of the machine from one instruction to the next. The trick for the halting problem is to know whether any particular Turing Machine is going to stop or not.

Though the steps in his proof become a bit technical, Turing went on to introduce a *universal* machine into the picture, one capable of imitating any of the simpler machines. It's a master algorithm. Turing set it the task—the hypothetical task—of computing every natural number, in however many ways that might be accomplished. This was typical of the careful way Turing built purely theoretical models, but applies nonetheless to any conceivable *real* machine with a finite number of ways of expressing its output. As it turns out, the

Universal Turing Machine can't decide whether it will stop or not; it can't really exist. Perfectly computable natural numbers are obtained which no master algorithm can generate. Therefore, no *general* method (*i.e.* the universal machine) for deciding whether a given Turing Machine will stop can be had.

Turing's thoroughly original vision of a problem which, after all, had already been famously solved produced some very clear thinking about what computing is, what algorithms do, and how physically to organize the procedure. In this sense, a modern computer is sometimes called a Universal Turing Machine, though obviously without being warranted to decide the undecidable. Turing established, as well, a formal equivalence among machines that proceed multiply, in parallel, or in simple sequence—a finite number of internal states is still a finite number. (Of course, there isn't a theoretical luxury of time in real problems; some ways of designing machines are more useful than others.)

Whether Turing would stand by his own test for consciousness today is unknowable; perhaps he thought the terms of the question unduly confining, as if consciousness were not of one universal kind. He may well have believed, as he once remarked, that beyond a certain stage, "we shan't know how it does it."

Already it's becoming difficult to judge the performance of computers: At least one famous mathematical proof, of the "Four-Color Problem," exists only in computer-generated form. The actual computational labor would tax human patience and resources. The number of such proofs is growing, amounting to thousands of man-year equivalents; how can such a proof be checked? Is it a proof at all if only another computer can fully review it? When these computers disagree, and they occasionally do, who is to find the cause? The situation is a little dicey and apt to grow more so.

The Analytical Engine

Before the twentieth century, mechanical computing hadn't made any significant advances over the abacus, a versatile machine, to be sure. But with the abacus, a skilled operator must be "plugged in" to the computational process, carrying out each step and interpreting results. Invention of the slide rule certainly didn't eliminate the need for engaging a human mind in every calculation, though its principle of operation differs in a basic way from that of an abacus.

Slide rules work by representing numerical magnitudes with analogous physical quantities, by marking off lengths proportional to numbers (logarithms, in this case) and adding or subtracting those lengths to mimic the same operations of arithmetic. Such devices, called *analog*, abound in the everyday business of measurement, from ancient water clocks equating flow to the passage of time, to multi-dialled contraptions in which the angles and speeds of cams, gears, and levers grind out a series of appropriately scaled results.

The abacus, by contrast, is nothing like a continuous flow of water or a rotating gear wheel. It calculates with individual beads, which get shifted around a bit but which are still transparently numbers. Nothing has been translated into degrees of rotation, voltages, flow, or whatever, to make a problem run toward its solution. An abacus is a *digital* device.

At any rate, calculation remained a purely human activity, with occasional mechanical assists, until the English mathematician Charles Babbage turned his mind to getting the infuriating, humanly-tabulated errors out of mathematical tables. Babbage drew up blueprints for a hand-cranked analog device around 1833. His Difference Engine No. 1 is the first automatic calculator for solving problems beyond simple addition. Or, to be exact, in its constructed form, the first 25 percent of a fully automatic calculator. Babbage couldn't afford to build it and persuaded the British government to fund a working model. When checks stopped coming, he had about 2,000 assembled brass parts and no prospects. The disappointment might have been greater except that he'd already begun design of a more powerful machine he called the Analytical Engine, which would accomplish a great deal more than the ordinary operations of arithmetic. Babbage, in fact, anticipated in one great swoop most of the requirements for a truly modern, all-purpose computer. To begin, he divided the machine's working areas (all purely mechanical!) into "store" and "mill," effectively memory and processor. Input and partial results moved according to a set of master instructions, like a program, which must first be entered into the Engine. Babbage envisioned setting up programs by means of punched cards—a simple form of which, he may have seen used in the Jacquard loom. The machine's output might be printed, punched, or plotted as needed.

Given a program to organize any sequence of manipulations within the Engine, the input might consist of anything at all—numbers, letters, or otherwise defined symbols. The advance in thinking, from mere calculators to real computers, was complete in Babbage's new concept. But this machine, too, wasn't constructed. Babbage died after a full career of frustration in advancing a technology before its time. Difference Engine No. 1 did eventually get built by some interested scientists and tinkerers—unveiled in 1991—mostly as a tribute to his memory, but also to find out whether it works. It does, and with only the slightest corrections to its voluminous, labyrinthine plans.

Linus Pauling (1901-1994)

In the heady days when quantum theory was coming together—even as the basic equations were being set down in 1926 and 1927—an American postdoctoral fellow kept showing up in all the best labs, including those of Sommerfeld, Bohr, and Schrödinger. Linus Pauling had just completed his chemistry doctorate at California Institute of Technology in 1925. Pauling's compendious and original mind was, in very short order, to put chemistry on a new, quantum footing, infusing the subject with that mix of heightened clarity and uncertainty which mathematical equations always seem to entail.

As Pauling himself would point out later, he happened to be the only person around at the time who had a thorough knowledge of both chemistry and quantum theory. In fact, the amount of physical chemistry he seemed able to keep rattling around in his head amazed colleagues throughout his career. When Pauling advocated, later in life, the benefits of taking large doses of vitamin C, sales of ascorbic acid were bound to rise. It did not matter that studies appeared to show mostly neutral results: No prudent person would want to be in the position of outguessing Pauling. He enjoyed a deserved reputation for being a decade or two ahead of his peers.

Chemistry For a New Era

His first contributions described a new way of understanding the chemical bond, the electric force that holds elements together as molecules. Chemistry, by the way, is fundamentally the study of the behavior of the few outermost electrons circling an atomic nucleus; nothing else really matters. From this rather constrained set of initial conditions arise endless configurations—chemical compounds—which account for pretty much everything there is.

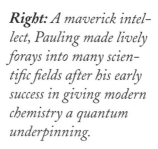

Right: A maverick intellect, Pauling made lively forays into many scientific fields after his early success in giving modern chemistry a quantum underpinning.

All intact atoms are officially neutral, having the same number of protons and electrons. That doesn't mean, however, that the electrons most distant from the nucleus can't feel an attraction for other nuclei. Substances have a certain electronic "look," depending on how well those last few orbiting negative charges (electrons) mask the positive charges residing at the center of things, in the nucleus. An electron or two veering out of exclusive orbit around its own nucleus to include a neighbor is the electric girdle of force that holds molecules together.

Pauling invented a very practical concept, the electronegativity scale, to rate as a single number the relative abilities of elements to attract electrons into more or less shared orbits. A single glance at one of Pauling's charts shows, for example, that fluorine has the strongest pull (4.0), cesium and short-lived francium the weakest (0.7). This variation was hardly news to chemists, but the scale simplified the discussion considerably. It also allowed for a smooth progression of possible bond strengths and types from equitable sharing of charge (covalent) to near complete dispossession (ionic). The ideas are collected in *The Nature of the Chemical Bond* (1939), easily the most influential work in chemistry of the twentieth century.

The Theory of Resonance

Actually, Pauling had arrived at the chemical bond and deeper findings much earlier. By 1929, he had worked out his major thesis—that *resonance* is among the possible bond states and is present in many compounds. With the conventional means of describing chemical bonds, some very common situations had to be glossed over (like the distance between carbon and oxygen atoms in carbon dioxide). Carbon can share the influence of four electrons—which makes it an unusually popular and versatile element in a compound. If it allocated two each (a double bond) to two oxygens, the distance between carbon and oxygen should be 1.22 Å. But it's not; it's 1.16 Å, which argues for a stronger bond, a triple (leaving only a single for the remaining oxygen). How to understand this?

Pauling, of course, had a quantum feeling for things. If both bonding arrangements are possible, then both will happen, and in the quantum way of things, they can't be definitely separated. The two states resonate back and forth indistinguishably, resulting in a bond that is neither one nor the other. It's stronger than the double-double possibility and a little weaker than a strict triple-single description. Bonds like this don't always crop up—some molecules only have one mode to "choose" from—but where there is an ambiguity of choice, resonance between states will occur.

Left: The famous DNA double helix: the honor of discovery belongs to Francis Crick and James Watson; clues as to its chemical nature and shape were provided by Pauling.

143

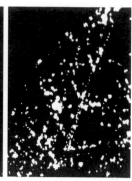

Right: Autoradiographs of an asphalt shingle, and a random leaf (far right) picked up in Troy, New York, thirty-six hours after a 1953 nuclear test in Nevada. The self-exposed plates demonstrate the presence of fallout (by rain) even on the opposite side of the continent to the explosion site.

Below: Through the 1950s and '60s, Pauling spent as much time pursuing anti-nuclear and peace campaigns as in research. The government placed whatever obstacles it could in his path.

Resonating electrons are of the approved quantum pattern—cloudy smears of probability. Orbits are shadings of likelihood, here darker, there lighter, for finding any electrons. The possible states for a given molecular system most resemble, then, wave mechanical equations drawn up according to quantum principles.

With this method of calculating bond lengths and angles, chemistry makes a good deal more sense. The numbers come out right, for one thing, and better predictions are possible for novel molecular combinations. Though the quantizing of chemistry was welcomed everywhere, a bizarre development in the late 1940s took it off the list of permissible ways of doing chemistry in the then Soviet Union. One Gennadi Chelintsev, fittingly enough a professor of chemical warfare, published a tirade entitled, "On a Machist Theory in Chemistry and Its Propagandists." For "Machist" read "artificial" or "idealistic tinkering," something that appears to work but only through hollow agreements within its own terms. Ernst Mach's scientific phi-

losophy had been identified by Soviet dialecticians as the root of error in non-Marxist science. Central committees met, rejected Chelintsev, rejected resonance, kept quantum theory, and generally hedged enough bets to preserve both chemistry and social theorists in working condition.

Breakthrough in Biochemistry

Pauling, meanwhile had moved on. Turning his attention to the molecular basis of life, he characterized the stages by which proteins degenerate—findings prompted by his study of hemoglobin in the 1930s. By 1940 he had proposed, with Max Delbruck, an immune system model in

which antibodies lock onto invading antigens through a special chemical "fit" between them. He declined participation in the atomic bomb project during World War II, but contributed improvements to conventional explosives. In peacetime, he returned to biochemistry, often working with Richard Corey, analyzing the structures of amino acids and polypeptides that make up proteins. He demonstrated for the first time in 1949, how a mutant gene is responsible for producing an altered form of a protein, thus causing a genetic defect (in his first example, the variant hemoglobin molecule of sickle-cell anemia).

He pioneered important techniques in the course of protein research, especially in adopting electrophoresis to separate huge, complex organic molecules into instantly readable component parts. (This method pulls molecules apart with electrical attraction, dragging individual segments through different distances in a thick gel.) He was among the first to use electron and X-ray diffraction analysis—bouncing beams off molecules set out in regular, crystal-like arrays and studying the patterns of reflection. His methods are now basic to the science. Using X-ray diffraction, he was the first to recognize a helical, or spiral,

structure in some large proteins (this insight guided researchers in looking for the molecular form of DNA, the famous double helix described in 1953).

No More War
Pauling's intellect and energy were by no means wholly consumed by chemistry—

he got a Nobel Prize for that in 1954. The Nobel Peace Prize in 1962 recognized his public role in pressing for a cessation of atmospheric nuclear testing. By the time a 1963 treaty suspended the practice, slightly over 300 bombs had been exploded on the earth's surface, injecting several hundred million curies of radiation into the atmosphere. After a test in Nevada, a random leaf picked up in New York could light up a photographic negative like a Christmas tree. And, of course, people around the world, but especially children, were absorbing unhealthy amounts of radioactive strontium-90 into their bones. Edwin Teller maintained this level of exposure couldn't shorten the average human life (worldwide) by more than two days. Pauling translated the same data to mean that about 15,000 lives a year would be ended prematurely.

Pauling condensed his views and research into a highly popular book, *No More War*, published in 1958. His efforts to make the nation aware of the consequences of nuclear testing paid off, at least insofar as the scientific line had to be rescripted. He relentlessly attacked the solacing idea that radiation exposure has no significant effects below certain "threshold" amounts—the concept remains controversial today after a great deal of research. In a debate with physicist W.F. Libby in 1958 (on Edward R. Murrow's "See It Now" television program), he ran into a solid wall of agreement on the hazards, disease, and mortality of weapons testing—the government simply maintained such a toll is acceptable. On balance, the public thought not.

The U.S. government disliked him heartily, only reissuing his revoked passport at the last minute to allow him to accept his 1954 prize in Sweden. During the 1970s, he was honored just about everywhere but in Washington. (The Soviet government had patched things up, dialectic and resonance magnanimously forgotten, with a Lenin Peace Prize in 1972.) Pauling's scientific work continued, and even in his nineties his unorthodox theories still raised the occasional stir.

Molecular Messages

Finding the right molecular description of DNA turned into one of history's horse races: Everyone figured Pauling and Corey would win. But neither they nor Rosalind Franklin and Maurice Wilkins got there first—James Watson and Francis Crick did, in the spring of 1953, using Franklin's excellent diffraction pictures of Wilkins' DNA crystals (getting DNA to settle into a nicely repeated configuration is a considerable challenge). They all owed a large conceptual debt to Pauling, who had discovered helical structures in proteins; but then, his chances of winning the DNA race were hampered by the lack of a passport that would allow him to attend conferences on the subject. So the discovery does have its dramatic elements. Crick, Watson, and Wilkins came away with the 1962 Nobel Prize and, had she lived, Franklin would undoubtedly have been in that company.

All this is astonishing given that no one could say for certain that DNA carried genetic information until 1944. It was known that DNA contained only four kinds of amino acid (guanine, adenine, cytosine, thymine), conjectured to repeat in an unvarying pattern. This seemed too simple a candidate to express a complete animal blueprint. An ingenious series of experiments by Avery, MacLeod, and McCarty ruled out other cellular components by trying to swap infective ability between two related bacterial strains. Tests with proteins and carbohydrates led nowhere. DNA, however, wrought a complete transformation. It had to be the genetic material.

A later experiment, by Erwin Chargaff and Ernst Vischer, established that DNA has a good deal more character than previously assumed: adenines and thymines always occurred in equal numbers, as did guanines and cytosines, but the two pairings came up in widely different proportions in the DNA of various species. Had molecular biologists been up on information theory, they may have set more store by the simplicity of DNA's constituents. Messages and information become more reliable as the number of "signal" elements decreases: more elements, more mistakes. The error rate also drops a bit if there's more than one signal for the same message. As it turns out, DNA is "read" in groups of three along its chain, with several repeated meanings expressed in its limited, four-character (CGAT) alphabet. Presumably, less efficient message systems have long since garbled themselves out of existence.

THE TRIPLET CODE FOR DNA

| FIRST POSITION | SECOND POSITION | | | | THIRD POSITION |

	T	C	A	G	
T	PHE	SER	TYR	CYS	T
	PHE	SER	TYR	CYS	C
	LEU	SER	STOP	STOP	A
	LEU	SER	STOP	TRP	G
C	LEU	PRO	HIS	ARG	T
	LEU	PRO	HIS	ARG	C
	LEU	PRO	GLN	ARG	A
	LEU	PRO	GLN	ARG	G
A	ILE	THR	ASN	SER	T
	ILE	THR	ASN	SER	C
	ILE	THR	LYS	ARG	A
	MET	THR	LYS	ARG	G
G	VAL	ALA	ASP	GLY	T
	VAL	ALA	ASP	GLY	C
	VAL	ALA	GLU	GLY	A
	VAL	ALA	GLU	GLY	G

Left: A DNA triplet (a combination of three of the four component amino acids—T, C, A, and G—in a given sequence) is a code for one of twenty other amino acid components in the step-by-step assembly of proteins. For example, the DNA triplet combinations T-T-A, T-T-G, C-T-T, etc, are each codes for leucine (LEU). The combinations T-A-A, T-G-A, and T-A-G are codes for ending the amino acid chain (STOP). A certain amount of redundancy (several codes indicating the same outcome) in the DNA "dictionary" lowers the chance of damage from random errors.

Stephen Hawking [1942-]

Earth is a privileged platform from which to observe and wonder about the universe. We're well removed from the center of things, far out on a trailing arm of a large spiral galaxy, the Milky Way. If we circled a more cosmopolitan star, closer in to the galactic core, a permanently luminous sky would bleach out the faint long-travelling lights by which we have gauged, as best we can, the scale and composition of the universe.

New Frontiers in Cosmology

The picture is still evolving. Remarkable advances in fundamental physical theory (chiefly relativity and quantum mechanics) have pushed inquiry into realms where the old Newtonian writ simply doesn't run. Adventurers in the field make up a *Who's Who* of top-level physics—from Alpher to Zeldovich—but none with more con-sistent freshness and unsuspected insights than Stephen Hawking.

Hawking believes himself lucky in most respects: he is, after all, a lineal successor to Newton as Lucasian Professor of Mathematics at Cambridge University, exploring the very nature of the universe. However, he contracted ALS (the motor-neuron disease also known as Lou Gehrig's disease) in the 1960s; he has contributed his finest work from a wheelchair, in conditions of increasing isolation. With progressive debility, Hawking can put his ideas across only with electronic assistance—keyboard and voice simulator. That such a flood of thought must be channelled into so precarious a trickle is not the kindest, or luckiest, of ironies. His formidable spirit commands as much admiration as his intellect.

Would-be cosmologists must ask themselves such questions as how did the uni-

Below: The galaxy Andromeda, about two hundred million suns, is part of the Local Group, a cluster of thirty galaxies and nebulae that includes the Milky Way. It's actually moving closer to our galaxy at a current speed of 110,000 miles per hour (180,000 km/h); arrival expected in roughly ten billion years.

verse begin, what is it doing now, and where does it all lead? Observation and hypothesis argue for an explosive beginning, the "big bang," somewhere between ten and twenty billion years ago. Galaxies of stars formed in the aftermath, streaming outward, and they are still rushing headlong—galaxies halfway to the observable rim are moving away at about 300 million miles per hour. Like a slow explosion, the universe seems to grow by 5 to 10 percent every billion years. It's been suggested that the cosmos continues to create itself,

popping matter into existence in the widening voids between galaxies, a "steady state" universe. Expansion could continue forever, but this view doesn't have much support at present. Instead, theorists prefer to investigate clues that bear on the limits of expansion: can the universe continue to enlarge itself or must it, in the end, be contracted by gravity to a "big crunch"?

The answer depends on too many unknowns. How much matter is there in the universe? A good estimate of all that is visible amounts to approximately 10^{80}

particles. A generous number, but not enough gravitating mass to account for the perceived slowness of universal expansion. Physicists speak of "missing matter," which is to say, the 70 to 90 percent that should be there and isn't detectable. Trial balances are tried with "dark matter," "strange matter," and "transmuted energy" (theory may allow that *neutrinos*—immensely abundant, immensely aloof—spontaneously turn into electrons). As yet, the sums don't work out.

The Elusive Constant

Haunting all discussion of expansion, or future contraction, is a concept bequeathed by Einstein: the cosmological constant. It's a term with which the unmanifested energy of the void—empty space—may be figured into the overall picture of the universe. A positive constant would work toward continued expansion, a negative term would retard or reverse it. No experimental value for a cosmological constant has been found; elegant theories are wrecked by it. Yet something very like this constant *must* occur in a unified description. To explain observed expansion, at least in part, physicists have gone so far as to posit a fifth fundamental force, rather antigravitational in effect, but experimental searches lend no support. More promising for evaluating energy density of the vacuum are effects associated with the "Higgs field," a decidedly abstruse piece of quantum conjecture.

In much the same way as the *photon* (a *boson*) mediates, and thus defines, electromagnetic phenomena, a Higgs boson gives rise to the properties of mass. Its corresponding field is helpful in describing energy conditions in the vacuum. But as so often happens in cosmology, the evidence is wobbly, Higgs is unconfirmed. The journals are strewn with castoffs: supergravity, antigravity, deflated symmetries, unified theories. Any one of them might be instantly reconditioned, should the facts warrant.

Ten Billion Light Years and Beyond

Expanding, contracting, or all done with mirrors, an inventory of what can be seen is still useful: Persistent observation of the heavens, with optical and radio instruments, discloses a universe populated by several billion billion stars, clumped by the billions into galaxies, which, in turn, group themselves loosely by the thousands into discernible clusters and even superclusters. It's a large universe, too, and pretty evenly spread out, *isotropic*. What we can see of it extends perhaps ten billion light years in every direction. The ultimate boundary hasn't been set, first because such a thing may not exist—at least not in a conventional maplike sense—and secondly because any signal from the edge has little theoretical or practical chance of reaching detectors.

The engine that runs the universe is gravity. Hydrogen, the main constituent everywhere, helium, and scant amounts of heavier elements tug each other into nebulous clouds, out of which the stars condense. When enough gaseous mass comes together, gravitational pressure causes ignition: tightly confined hydrogen atoms collide with ever higher velocities and begin to fuse, creating helium and a great deal of free energy. The same reaction can be packaged as a thermonuclear, or fusion, bomb. A fission bomb acts as the trigger, providing enormous pressures, if only for a few millionths of a second. But hydrogen bombs are messy, touch-and-go affairs; stars, once turned on, may shine for billions of years.

Star Lifetimes

The surprising stability of stars reflects a balance of the forces at work within them. Gravity pushes matter inward, while the energy of collisions drives atoms apart. The diameter of any star is precisely the equilibrium size at which eruptive and compressive tendencies hold each other in check. Were the amount of interior energy to drop, gravity would predominate for a while, shrinking a star's circumference until opposing forces match up again. Such adjustments, though carried out very smoothly, occur inevitably through a star's life cycle. Gravity goes on forever, but fuel does not. Hydrogen "burns" to form helium, helium begets lithium, and so forth, each stage producing less energy until finally—for a large star—the fusion of silicon yields elemental iron. Fusing iron would yield no energy at all (in fact the process consumes energy). How a star dies as it reaches the end of its fuel depends on such things as the mass it started with, its relative elemental composition, and the intensity with which it burned.

Not all the gravitational sweepings gathered up in space can "turn on," like stars. Accumulations of old star matter, rich in heavier elements, become planets and planetoids. Insufficiently dense gaseous concentrations will remain stunted "brown stars" until more fuel is gathered in. Successfully ignited stars range in size from somewhat smaller than our own sun to several hundred times its mass. Factors

governing energy output place limits on star lifetimes, from a mere hundred million years for certain massive examples to ten billion or more for other types. (Sol is in middle age, with an expectancy of another five billion years or so.) Understanding the kinds of celestial hulks that used-up stars may leave behind has revolutionized our view of the universe.

Gravity is relentless. When a star shuts down, one of several cataclysms must follow. Stars of masses comparable to Sol, after throbbing for a while as *red giants*, fall inward to diameters of a few thousand miles. Matter at such pressure and density (several hundred tons per cubic inch) can bear up only through repulsive forces between electrons; the star radiates intensely for a while as a *white dwarf* before "turning off" and growing cold. Should a white dwarf orbit with a companion star, hydrogen drawn in from its neighbor may fuse in the dramatic pyrotechnic called a *nova*.

Stars of about two to five solar masses may stoke themselves long enough to start producing large amounts of iron. As the

Left: A 1987 supernova erupting in the Large Magellanic Cloud. Astronomers would expect to find at its core an exotic remnant, either a neutron star or a black hole. Heavier elements expelled in the cataclysm can coalesce over time to form planets.

These pages: A computer simulation of stages in the evolution of a black hole. Its growth, through the one-way passage of matter across its event horizon, may be retarded or even reversed by a curious quantum mechanism first postulated by Stephen Hawking: A disjoining of particle/ antiparticle pairs in the black hole's immediate neighborhood leads to an apparent radiation of energy from the black hole. A net loss of mass and consequent—very slow—evaporation of the singularity result when outflow exceeds inflow. In the later stages—as in the lower far right picture—the outflow (indicated in the simulation's vertical dimension) becomes greater than the inflow (shown in the horizontal dimension).

critical point is passed, an astounding collapse—measured in mere minutes—compresses the center to a radius of ten miles or so while explosively dispersing hot star matter in a *supernova*. What's left, at the core, cannot support itself even with electron pressure and falls into an even more degenerate state in which electrons and protons are forced together as neutrons. Densities here reach several million tons per cubic inch—the limit for any kind of matter recognizable as such. A neutron star's rotation and magnetic field interact with infalling matter to send jets of energy outward. Seen from the right perspective, it flashes like a lighthouse, but in the radio region of the spectrum. The first observations of these regular, seemingly intelligent signals (in 1967) prompted the name *LGMs*, for "little green men." We now believe these *pulsars* to be neutron stars.

That leaves, of course, the fate of even larger stars. Their collapse brings on not only a physical but a theoretical crisis. Ultimately, gravity compresses with a force so powerful that even light cannot escape; these stars become *black holes*. It's meaningless to ask what lies inside: no theory holds up beyond the *event horizon,* the boundary that confines light. Such objects, or non-objects, had emerged in calculations made by astronomer Karl Schwarzschild in 1916, mere weeks after looking at Einstein's new field equations for gravity. Solutions showed gravity might, under special circumstances, so radically warp surrounding space as to form a closed loop, a

singularity. Nothing may be said about the size of a singularity nor of the nature of time or matter within. The very concepts vanish into the singularity, along with notions of causality and probability.

The Mysterious Black Hole

Theorists including Chandrasekhar, Landau, and J. Robert Oppenheimer considered black holes during the 1930s. In 1965, Penrose showed that massive stars *must* disappear into black holes. By 1970 Hawking had enlarged the conclusion to encompass the beginnings of the universe: if we grant only that general relativity is correct, then the universe originated in a big bang singularity. In the years since, Hawking has performed much of the intellectual exploration at the black hole's perimeter. As he has demonstrated, black holes may interact with surrounding space in an odd way.

Particle/antiparticle pairs (*virtual particles*) should appear in large numbers in the roiled, stressed vacuum near a black hole. One of the pair might easily fall through the event horizon before annihilating its twin, whose direction may take it clear of the singularity. Thus, the black hole appears to radiate energy; indeed, the disappearing twin can presumably still combine with an appropriate antiparticle within the black hole to yield a net reduction in mass. Black holes must have, then, a very subtle tendency to "evaporate." Hawking himself had wondered why there seemed to be no microscopic black holes

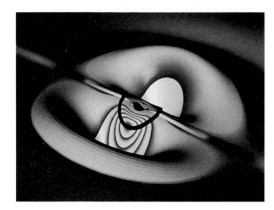
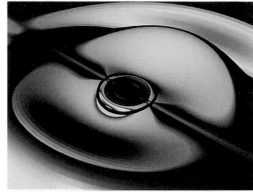

whizzing around. Big bang pressures in the first trillionth of a second should have turned out quite a few "primordial" black holes—even atom-sized things weighing as much as a mountain. Taking radiative evaporation into account, however, eliminates primordial singularities of mass less than about a billion tons; the smaller ones have by now dissipated themselves.

Not only do black holes "shine" by quantum processes, they are apt to steal matter from all parts of their gravitational vicinity, from nearby stars or nebular concentrations. Should a black hole be spinning, particles will spiral in toward the event horizon losing energy and forming a very bright *accretion disk* around a black hole's equator. Such secondary scintillation indicates the probable existence of a black hole. Indeed, certain very distant sources, radiating at incomprehensible power, seem explicable only in terms of hugely engorged black holes—massing, in extreme cases, as much as a hundred million suns. They've been named *quasars*, quasistellar radio sources. One such object, of about a hundred thousand solar masses, appears to be tearing things apart at the center of our own galaxy.

With black holes pretty comfortably established, physicists formulated extremes of mathematical test conditions to see what happens when you play with a black hole. If it were rotating and ever-so-slightly deformed, or perhaps dancing orbitally with another black hole, might the event horizon become so distorted that we could glimpse its insides? Will we find such "naked singularities"? Certain views suggest that paths may be chosen through a suitably deformed event horizon that lead incalculably to more distant points in space or time. For any real life form, the track would have to lie in some region where gravitational forces nicely cancel out; in such an intense field, the variation in attractive strength from, say, head to toe—*tidal force*—pulls matter apart.

As to the event horizon itself, the warping of light leads to strange perceptions. Modelling the situation, with properly twisted coordinates, shows that travellers located precisely at the horizon get a backward picture versus the view of an outside observer; outward and inward appear reversed. Should the travellers plunge (fatally) through the horizon, a future wayfarer may still see them waving an infinitely slow goodbye. The image is stuck on the horizon, smeared out across time. The last photons, the ones that would have depicted their disappearance, can't escape from the black hole.

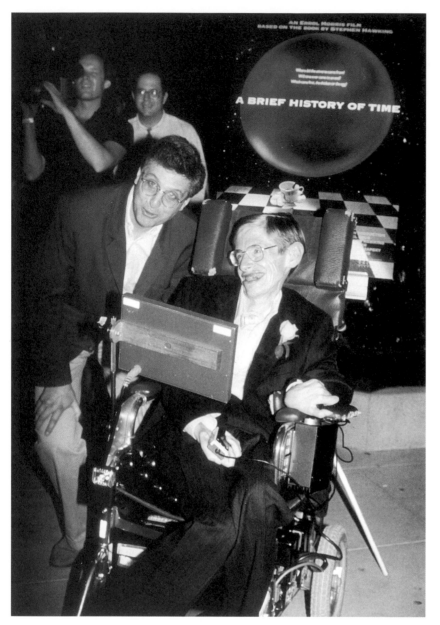

A BRIEF HISTORY OF TIME

But even black holes, as seen from outside, have a finite extension and mass. It's important only to notice here how the black hole, with measurable content and size, has no boundary. It really hasn't; not as far as anyone inside could ever discover.

A boundless but finite space, red-shifting outward motion, light making great circles in the cosmos—this begins to sound familiar, very close to a universe with which we have had dealings. Do we live in a black hole, or something very like one? What's outside? Are the skins of singularities just separations between universes? Might the big bang have been an irruption into time of a singularity from "somewhere else"? What if the bang happened so fast that some regions lost light contact with each other: could there be "bubble" universes next door? These questions legitimately arise in modern cosmology. Some part of the answer is probably *yes*, but we don't know which parts because this fascinating set of questions seems to require a cosmologist who is simultaneously in and out of the universe making observations.

Time Before Time

Clearly, as Hawking saw, physics of this sort has a great deal to say about the way things started off in the universe. His own thinking has been directed at smoothing out those parts which are reasonably connectable to *our* universe. Working with other keen minds, he demonstrated that giving the universe a quantum wave function leads in some instances to a beginning of time that doesn't really begin. It's a quantum imaginary time with an indiscernible boundary that "collapses" into ordinary time—one would like to say soon after the initial cosmic flaring, but the word "soon" can have no meaning in imaginary time. Suffice it to say that as the primordial energy unleashed itself, with its featureless homogeneity and symmetry already broken, time started.

Above: Astronomically speaking, it's an event somewhat rarer than a supernova, but theoretical physicists do get into the movies once in a great while. Hawking poses here in Beverly Hills with Errol Morris, director of A Brief History of Time, *based on Hawking's bestselling book about his career and work in cosmology.*

If an imaginary observer could indeed watch events from the interior of a black hole, how would things look? For one thing, light travelling outward would redshift as gravity retarded its progress. It could never reach the horizon, though it might spend an eternity making the trip. To the observer it seems the ever fainter, redder light is traversing vast distances. Light rays not aimed directly outward will be gently bent back toward their origins, eventually making wide, long loops in the interior. Judging from the images reaching him, our observer concludes that the space around him is vast and boundless.

Birth of a Universe

osmology, ancient as the human mind, appears to concern itself with obscure propositions about patient turtles and morose giants bearing earth across time and an occasionally miraculous firmament. We have always had, apparently, the cultural leisure to speculate on the end of days or the endless cycling of them, on the distance to paradise or the size of the wolf, Fenris, that ate the world.

It is only within the last fifty years that science has proceeded coherently and earnestly to construct testable, or potentially testable, narrations of the cosmic origin. Physicists tread lightly among the ultimate questions of being, for there are few scientific reasons to prefer any explanation over any other. When theorists *must* bring matter into existence, as in the case of virtual particles, they pointedly snuff them out within a nanobreath, restoring nothingness to near pristine form and avoiding messier issues altogether.

Edwin Hubble's discovery in the 1930s that galaxies everywhere are fleeing outward, away from one another, suggested to physicists, George Gamow in particular, a condition that must have originated in a single, long-past explosion, the hypothetical "big bang." Current speeds and distribution of galaxies argue for a cataclysmic event between, say, ten and twenty billion years ago. Penzias and Wilson confirmed, in 1964, an important byproduct predicted of the big bang: the near uniform presence in the universe of hydrogen that is still cooling from the initial blow-up. Moreover, this hydrogen debris has dropped by now to an estimated temperature of 2.7° Kelvin. It emits radio waves, making up the so-called "background radiation" or "universal background" (an unusual discovery in that the

theorists hadn't mentioned what they were looking for to the experimentalists, who were more interested at the time in getting the nuisance background noise out of their microwave antennas).

Unhappily, most of the excitement in scientific cosmology takes place in a mathematical world so abstruse, namely gauge theory, that physical interpretations tend to be elusive, running from conjectural to baffling. Nonetheless, certain cosmological constructs—thinking particularly of black holes—have consistent theoretical basis and some observational support.

Current theories, leaning heavily toward quantum mechanical reconstructions of time's first trillionths of a second, are exquisitely sensitive to (expected) bumps and irregularities in the chaos of the primordial event. Forces as we know them (gravity, electromagnetism, strong and weak nuclear interactions) emerge from the quickly degrading homogeneity of a high-energy quantum soup, "breaking symmetry," and imparting to the universe its essential nature and direction, all before the universe had erupted to a globule one sextillionth of a centimeter across.

For the present, spectators to cosmology may guardedly engage in contemplation of such things as cosmic strings (massive fractures in the universe's dimensional structure, like internal cracks in a stressed ice cube), Higgs particles (with negative energy and a doomsday finality), multiple universes, and imaginary time. Nor is it known today whether the best sort of Grand Unified Theory (GUT) should nest our bare world of experience within an ultimate nine- or twelve- or thirteen-dimensional manifold. We *can* say with some assurance that a three- or four-dimensional glance doesn't penetrate far into the cosmological murk.

Glossary

acceleration: Rate of change of *velocity,* whether an increase or decrease and including motion along a curved path.

accretion disk: Whirling accumulation of infalling matter around a super-massive object such as a white dwarf, neutron star or black hole. Occurs only in binary systems, so that matter is drawn in from an orbiting companion, usually a normal star.

algorithm: A step-by-step procedure for solving any particular kind of mathematical problem.

allele: Any of the many variants of a specific gene.

analog: pertaining to similarity, as in constructing images of a problem or process in another medium, *e.g.,* as transforming numbers or functions into appropriately scaled voltages, mechanical motions, etc., or modelling sound as bumpy tracks in vinyl.

architecture (relating to computers): The plan or layout for operating on inputs, *i.e.,* by what steps information is shifted around, stored, and retrieved in processing.

atom: A configuration of elementary particles that makes up the smallest, and characteristic, unit of a chemical element. It consists of electrons circulating around a nucleus of protons and neutrons (except for hydrogen, the simplest, whose commonest form contains an electron and proton only).

baryon: A relatively heavy elementary particle, like the proton or neutron, both about 1,836 times more massive than the electron, which is a "lepton" (lightweight). Baryons are *fermions.*

big bang: In cosmological theory, the eruption of everything in the present universe from a compact, pointlike state about ten to fifteen billion years ago.

black hole: A region in which huge gravitational forces prevent escape of matter (even of light itself). Certain massive stars may collapse into such a "degenerate" state.

blue shift: Shortening of light wavelength, *i.e.,* increase in frequency, as perceived by observers moving toward one another.

boson: Any elementary particle with a whole-number spin (*e.g.,* +1, -1, +2, etc.), such as a *photon* or *meson.* These particles fulfill conditions computed by means of Bose-Einstein statistics and do not satisfy the *exclusion principle.*

commutivity: Mathematical property of any operation that works equivalently in mixed order, *e.g.,* in ordinary arithmetic 3 x 4 equals 4 x 3— thus multiplication is commutative.

complementarity: The condition, in quantum physics, that certain pairs of attributes—like position and momentum, or time and energy— share a degree of uncertainty in measurement; more precision in ascertaining one necessarily reduces accuracy in the other.

conditioned reflex: An involuntary behavior induced by environmental stimuli (cues such as sound, sights, etc.) not normally sufficient in themselves to produce such a reaction.

constant: In mathematics, an unchanging value, such as the ratio of a circumference to its diameter (*pi*) or the speed of light in a vacuum (*c*).

differentiation: The method, in calculus, for finding the rate of growth of a function at any point in its range.

dominant (trait): Of two forms of a gene present in an organism, the one actually expressed during growth and development; eye color, leaf shape, surface markings are common, observable examples.

Doppler effect: The apparent shifting of sound to higher or lower pitch as the source approaches or recedes from an observer; similarly, light increases or decreases in frequency depending on motion between observers.

electron: Elementary particle that carries the unit of negative electrical charge. It is a *fermion,* with mass only about $1/1836$ that of the *proton.*

electrophoresis: Analysis of substances by pulling chemical constituents through a viscous gel using the force of an electrical field. Various fractions travel at different rates, resulting over standardized time intervals in characteristically spaced bands seen in the gel.

entropy: Tendency of energy to become useless or, equivalently, of everything to run down, moving from states of greater order to lesser.

eugenics: The notion that species, most especially including humans, can and should be bred for "desirable" traits.

event horizon: A boundary in space from beyond which no light signal may reach any outside observer.

exclusion principle: First set out by Wolfgang Pauli (for electrons), the condition that no two like *fermions* (*e.g.,* two protons, two electrons) in an atom may occupy the same quantum level at the same time, *i.e.,* they may not have identical sets of *quantum numbers.*

fermion: An elementary particle with half-integral spin (*e.g.,* $+1/2$, $-1/2$, $+3/2$, etc.), such as a proton or electron. These particles fulfill conditions computed by means of Fermi-Dirac statistics and must satisfy the *exclusion principle.*

frame; "frame of reference": Any system of objects, observers, etc., all moving together relative to any other system.

frequency: Number of cyclic repititions per unit of time, as of electromagnetic waves, sound waves, etc.; often measured in cycles per second, or hertz.

function: A mathematically expressed relation between two or more variables, as in expressing, say, distance (*d*) in terms of the variables velocity (*r*) and time (*t*), *d=rt* or, stated more generally, distance is a function of rate and time, *d=f*(*r,t*).

ganglion, ganglia (pl.): A junction of many nerve fiber ends.

genotype: The kind of information for producing a living organism contained in its genes.

geodesic: Least-energy path between two points in *space-time.*

ground state: For any system of particles, especially an atom or molecule, its least-energy condition—no quantum shifts to a lower level being allowable.

group: In mathematics, a set of elements related by an operation that generates only members of the set. Groups must contain an *identity element* and an inverse (a "reversal") for every operation.

heterozygous: In genetics, having two forms (*alleles*) of a gene in a chromosome pair.

homozygous: In genetics, having identical forms (*alleles*) of a gene in a chromosome pair.

hypersurface: In mathematics, a geometric surface constructed in more than three dimensions, *i.e.,* with more than three coordinate numbers specifying any point. Not easily visualized, but manipulated by the usual analytic methods.

identity element: In a mathematical *group,* a member that changes nothing when combined with another in a group operation, *e.g.,* the number one leaves all other real numbers unchanged in multiplication; zero has that property in the operation of addition.

induction, magnetic: The property of a fluctuating magnetic field to cause flow of electric current in a conductor.

induction, mathematical: Method of proof by an implied, unending repetition of a procedure known to produce a true result in a chain of successors, *i.e.,* that for the same, "heritable" reason k, $k+1$, $k+2$…are true, so will $k+n$ be true.

inertia: Property of matter that resists *acceleration*.

integration: In calculus, a general method for finding the cumulative value of a function through some part of its range.

interval: In the context of fields (and thus in differential geometry), a way of characterizing the "distance" between two points that is unchanged by choice of coordinates; an invariant.

irrational number: A number that has no precise expression as a fraction, thus all unending, nonrepeating decimals; *e.g.,* $\sqrt{2}$, *pi*.

isotope: Form of a chemical element: though protons in any nucleus are a fixed number, neutrons are not. Generally all but one or two neutron numbers are unstable configurations for any particular element. Isotopes are specified by the sum of protons and neutrons in a nucleus, *e.g.,* Pu^{239}, Pu^{240}, etc.

isotropic: Evenly distributed.

light cone: In relativistic geometry, the range of future space-time within potential communication with an observer. Faster-than-light ("superluminal") signals—not allowed in theory—would be needed for knowledge of events outside a light cone.

mass: A measure of *inertia*.

matrix: In mathematics, an array of numbers or functional elements ordered in relation to one another so as to be manipulated and analyzed by matrix theorems concerning transformation and solution of problems.

meson: Term covering many different types of unstable elementary particles—a complex family of *bosons*, including members with positive, negative, and zero charge. Originally named for "middling" masses in the range 200 to 1,000 times that of the electron, though heavier ones are now included.

metric: In differential geometry, an expression of the rules of measure within a kind of geometry.

molecule: Two or more *atoms* joined in a stable configuration by electrical forces among them.

mutation: Substitution of one nucleic acid for another at any location along a gene segment in a DNA strand. May occur in the natural course of DNA production, at random, or through extrinsic action, as by chemicals or radiation.

natural selection: Evolutionary process described by Charles Darwin, by which species develop, thrive, or decline through suitability to take advantage of their environments; often summed up as "survival of the fittest."

neutrino: Elementary particle, a *boson* occurring in several guises, having scarcely any interaction with ordinary matter but perhaps the most abundant particle in the universe—estimated to outnumber *baryons* by a factor of ten billion times.

Up to 99% of the energy in a *supernova* is thought to be released in this near-undetectable form.

nova: Explosive event, often repetitive, associated with binary star systems in which one of the mutually orbiting bodies is a white dwarf or neutron star. Infalling matter from an *accretion disk* is thought to create some condition of energy criticality, with consequent eruptive release. About 25–75 nova events occur in a large galaxy per year.

pathogen: Any microbial or viral agent that causes disease in a living organism.

phenotype: The physical form of an organism; the physical expression of its *genotype*.

photon: A *boson*, the smallest unit of light; especially as in describing particle-like properties of light.

pi: Invariant ratio of any circle's diameter to its circumference; a transcendental number, $3.14159265\ldots$

prime number: Any number divisible only by itself and one.

proton: Elementary particle, a *fermion*, normally found in the atomic nucleus. It carries the unit of positive charge and is believed the most stable of all particles, with a half-life estimated at 10^{30} years—about a hundred trillion trillion years longer than the present age of the universe.

pulsar: An astronomical source of sharply periodic radio emissions; believed to be rotating neutron stars with jetlike interaction of ionized material at its poles.

quantum numbers: Simple coefficient values derived from quantum-mechanical equations describing a particle's energy state (usually a set of four—principal, spin, orbital, magnetic—but sometimes including "isospin").

quasar (quasi-stellar object): One of a class of extremely distant astronomical objects radiating immense amounts of energy. Although their nature is not known, likely explanations include enormous black holes interacting with substantial parts of galaxies.

recessive (trait): Of two forms of a gene present in an organism, one not actually expressed during growth and development; only if both *alleles* are recessive will a trait show in its recessive form.

red shift: Lengthening of light wavelength, *i.e.,* increase in frequency, as perceived by observers moving away from one another.

saddle point: In mathematics, especially the matrices of game theory, an intersection of two sets of functions at some shared value. In game theory, the coincidence of a maximum (*i.e.,* best) of all unfavorable outcomes with a minimum (*i.e.,* worst) of all favorable outcomes; the "minimax."

sensitized (to stimulus): Referring to behavior, having a *conditioned reflex* established.

singularities: The interior of a black hole, *i.e.,* a "place" outside the geometry of ordinary space-time, of which the physics is unknown. It may become a "naked singularity" if, by means only theoretically imaginable, its *event horizon* is pulled aside.

supernova: Especially large stellar explosion—briefly as bright as an entire galaxy—high in X-ray emission, sometimes leaving a core remnant in the form of a rapidly rotating neutron star. Believed to be somewhat rare, with perhaps only two to six occurences per century in a large galaxy.

tachyon: Name for any particle which, in theory only, travels faster than the speed of light. No evidence for such particles has been found.

uncertainty principle: The fundamental notion of quantum mechanics, as enunciated by Werner Heisenberg, that simultaneous and accurate determination of certain physical quantities is unobtainable by any means; such measurement is obscured through the very nature of matter and energy.

variable: In a mathematical *function*, an element, usually expressed as a letter (*x, y, z, etc.*), which may take on any prescribed value from a range of numbers or, indeed, other functions.

velocity: Rate of unaccelerated motion in a given direction. In physics, velocity always implies a direction; "speed" does not.

virtual particle: Fleeting existence of a particle-like state, imagined for theoretical reasons to occur in various energy transitions of stabler particles and fields. Virtual particles persist so briefly they are not, even in theory, directly observable.

virtual reality: Computer simulation, usually with three-dimensional and sound effects, of a genuine environment, device, process, etc. Such simulations are constructed so as to produce a realistic "feedback," creating observer participation in the illusion through shifting point of view, sound, effort/pressure, or other variable sensory cues.

wavelength: The distance from peak to peak of any energy form transmitted in regular, fluctuating cycles, like light and sound.

zero-sum (game): Any activity (a game, a business transaction, a division of resources) in which the net "stakes" can neither grow nor shrink, so that gains for one participant necessarily imply losses for others.

Scientific Notation and Units

NUMBERS AND PREFIXES

Very large or small numbers are usually expressed in an equivalent form in powers of ten, *e.g.,* 1,000,000 as 1×10^6; 0.00007 as 7×10^{-5}. Listed below are the standard prefixes for commonly used powers of ten and their symbols:

PREFIX	SYMBOL	MEANING
exa	E	$\times 10^{18}$
peta	P	$\times 10^{15}$
tera	T	$\times 10^{12}$
giga	G	$\times 10^9$
mega	M	$\times 10^6$
kilo	k	$\times 10^3$
hecto	h	$\times 10^2$
deca	da	$\times 10^1$
deci	. d	$\times 10^{-1}$
centi	c	$\times 10^{-2}$
milli	m	$\times 10^{-3}$
micro	μ	$\times 10^{-6}$
nano	n	$\times 10^{-9}$
pico	p	$\times 10^{-12}$
femto	f	$\times 10^{-15}$
atto	a	$\times 10^{-18}$

SOME PHYSICAL CONSTANTS

c	lightspeed in ideal vacuum	299,792.5 km/s
h	Planck's constant	6.626196×10^{-34} J/s
G	gravitational constant	6.673×10^{-11} Nm²/kg²
g	Earth gravity acceleration at Earth's surface	9.8 m/s² (32.2 ft/s²)

SI UNITS

Most units now in use are SI (Système International) units, derived from metric measures. Some commonly used measures and their equivalents are listed here:

UNIT	SYM	MEASURE	COMMENTS
meter	m	length	1 m equals 1.094 yards or 3.282 feet.
kilogram	kg	mass	1 kg equals 2.2 pounds.
second	s	time	defined as 9,192,631,770 vibrations in an atom of Cs¹³³.
kelvin	K	temperature	in centigrade degrees but starts from absolute zero, -213.16 °C.
ångstrom	Å	wavelength	10^{-10}m, or 0.1 nm.
volt	V	electricity	sufficient to produce 1 J/s of power potential.
newton	N	force	force that will accelerate 1kg mass at 1m/sec².
joule	J	energy	1 J equals the work of one newton through a distance of one meter.
curie	Ci	radiation	3.7×10^{10} disintegrations/second.
rad	rd	radiation dose	1 rd equals 0.01J of energy absorbed per kg.
rem		radiation dose	approx. equal to the rad for most radiation in the form of electrons or waves but adjusted upward for heavier particles to reflect higher potential for tissue damage.

Index

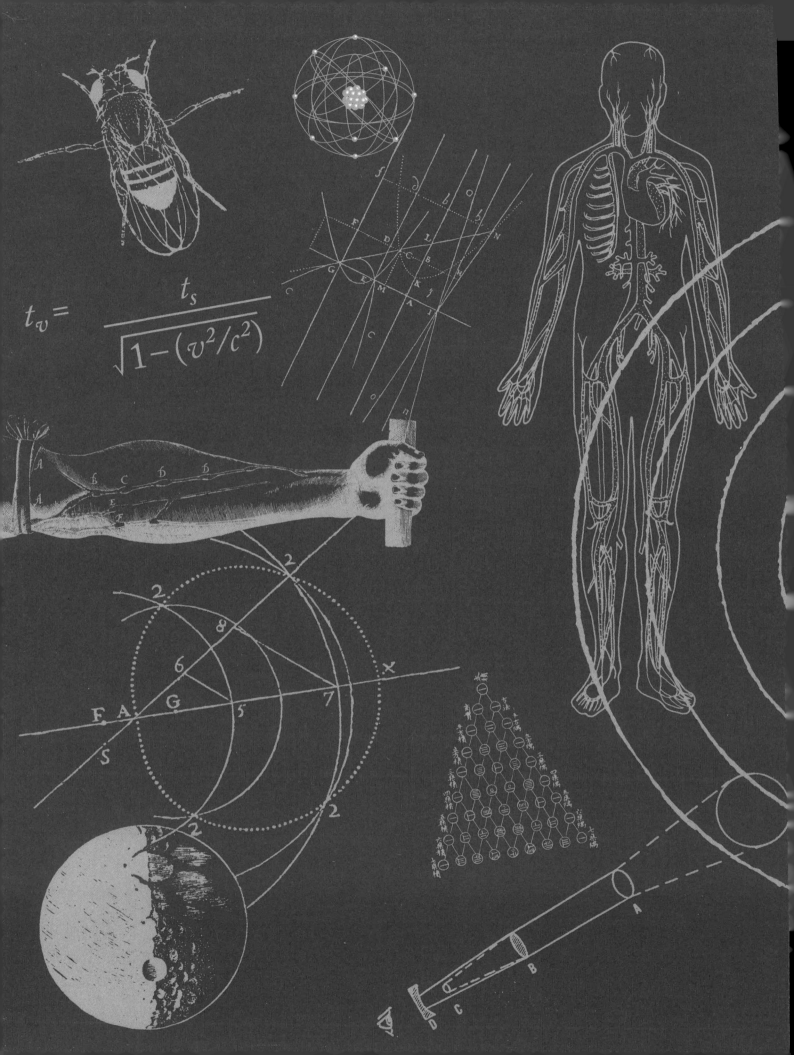

$$t_v = \frac{t_s}{\sqrt{1-(v^2/c^2)}}$$